Better Homes and Gardens®

STEP-BY-STEP
HOUSEHOLD
REPAIRS

BETTER HOMES AND GARDENS ® BOOKS
Editor: Gerald M. Knox
Art Director: Ernest Shelton
Managing Editor: David A. Kirchner

Building and Remodeling Editor: Joan McCloskey
Building Books Editor: Larry Clayton
Building Books Associate Editor: Jim Harrold

Associate Art Director (Managing):
  Randall Yontz
Associate Art Directors (Creative):
  Linda Ford, Neoma Alt West
Copy and Production Editors: Nancy Nowiszewski,
  Lamont Olson, Mary Helen Schiltz, David A. Walsh
Assistant Art Directors: Faith Berven, Harijs Priekulis
Senior Graphic Designer: Tom Wegner
Graphic Designers: Alisann Dixon, Lyne Neymeyer,
  Lynda Haupert, Bill Shaw, D. Greg Thompson,
  Mike Burns, Mike Eagleton, Deb Miner

Editor in Chief: Neil Kuehnl
Group Editorial Services Director: Duane Gregg
Executive Art Director: William J. Yates

General Manager: Fred Stines
Director of Publishing: Robert B. Nelson
Director of Retail Marketing: Jamie Martin
Director of Direct Marketing: Arthur Heydendael

Step-By-Step Household Repairs
Editors: Larry Clayton, Jim Harrold
Copy and Production Editor: Lamont Olson
Graphic Designers: Thomas Wegner, Mike Burns
Contributing Writer: David A. Kirchner
Technical Consultant: George Granseth
Drawings: Carson Ode

Acknowledgements
Our appreciation goes to the following
companies for contributing information
helpful in the preparation of this book.
Color Tile
Hawkeye Ceramic Tile Distributors, Inc.
Hi-Co Distributors
McDonald Glass and Glazing
Rock Island Millwork

CONTENTS

INTRODUCTION

There are many joys associated with being a homeowner: pride of ownership, financial security, and simple peace of mind to name just a few. But as you know, nothing is perfect, and you'll have ample proof of this as a homeowner. Things often break, malfunction, and wear out, and someone has to do the fixing or replacing.

Why roll up your sleeves when you could just as easily call a repairman? For one thing, it's not all that easy anymore. The simpler your repair, the less likely you are to find a repairman who's willing to make the trip to your house. If you do find one, you're almost certain to pay a premium price for his time and trouble. (It's not at all uncommon to have to pay $20 to $25 per hour for household repair work.)

Once you complete that first household repair—the one you were secretly worried about because you'd never done anything like it before—you'll realize a benefit that ranks right alongside convenience and cost. You'll know the satisfaction that comes with success at something you've done yourself. And as you become successful with more and more repairs, you may even start to feel more comfortable in your home because you'll be more in control of it.

If cost savings, convenience, or self-satisfaction is important to you, you're reading the right book. We've examined houses from top to bottom and inside out to come up with a sizable list of repair problems that most homeowners must deal with at some point. Then we conveniently grouped them into six sections to help you quickly find the repair information you need.

Leading off the book is a pictorial inventory of the basic tools you'll probably use. (Don't give up if all you own is a hammer and screwdriver. Buy special tools as you need them for a specific repair. They'll usually cost less than a repairman's services, and they'll be available the next time you need them.)

Our first two sections deal with "Walls and Ceilings" and "Floors and Stairs." If something around your house needs a cosmetic repair, you'll probably find it explained here. Whether it's patching nail holes in walls, quieting a squeaky stair tread, or replacing a tile in a ceramic tile floor, we show you how in step-by-step detail.

For more "functional" household repairs, check into the "Windows" and "Doors" chapters that follow. You'll find help for torn screens and broken glass, windows that won't open (or won't stay that way), and doors—all kinds of them—that squeak, bind, or cause other trouble.

Taking functional repairs one step further, our concluding pair of chapters deals with two of your home's systems—plumbing and electrical. If you've always thought these two systems were best left to professionals, you're in for some surprises. In "Electrical Repairs," we explain how you can safely troubleshoot a tripped circuit breaker or blown fuse, as well as how to repair or replace a variety of cords, receptacles, switches, and fixtures. Turn to the "Plumbing Repairs" chapter when you need to open a clogged drain, fix a leaky faucet, or tackle any of a host of other plumbing problems.

Repair Tools: The Basic Kit

Because time and use wear all things down, sooner or later something in your house will need fixing. When that happens, having the right tool for the job will speed things along considerably, while causing you to feel quite confident in your sundry skills as a full-fledged repairman. You already may have many of the tools shown here. Buy those you don't have on an as-needed basis. As with all tools, purchase the best quality you can afford, then take care of them.

General Repair Tools

Since so many repairs involve measuring and marking, *a flexible steel tape* is essential as is a *framing square* or a *combination square*.

To cut what you've measured, you'll need a *crosscut handsaw* for general-purpose cutting, a *keyhole saw* for cutting in tight quarters, and a *coping saw* for making intricate curves in thin material. Round out your cutting tool assortment with a *pocketknife* (not shown), a *utility knife*, and, if your budget permits, two power tool options: a 7¼-inch *circular saw* and a variable-speed *saber saw* (neither is shown here).

In a class by itself for all-around versatility is the *electric drill*. Choose a variable-speed, reversible model with a ⅜-inch chuck.

To drive and to remove a variety of fasteners, invest in a 16-ounce *curved-claw hammer*. For recessing finish nails, you'll need a *nail set* (buy several sizes). For more leverage when prying and removing fasteners, use a *pry bar*.

Purchase a set of *screwdrivers* in both slotted- and Phillips-head configurations.

Some household repairs require you to smooth wood surfaces. Use a *jack plane* for planing parallel to the grain, a *block plane* for cross-grain smoothing, and a *triangular file* for shaping metal surfaces.

Don't forget to pick up a couple of knives—a 6-inch *taping knife* for drywall work and an always-useful *putty knife*.

Electrical Repair Tools

You'll need surprisingly few tools to troubleshoot and correct electrical troubles, and those you need don't cost much. In addition to a couple of *screwdrivers*, you'll need *long-nose* and *lineman's pliers* to cut and twist wires, and to loop their ends to form connections.

In order to test electrical components for proper connections (with the power off), use a battery-operated *continuity tester*. Verify the presence or absence of electrical current (with the power on) with a *neon tester*. A *voltmeter* does both these jobs (with or without power), and also reads the voltage available at outlets.

Two other tools—a *fuse puller* for removing cartridge-type fuses if your system has them, and a *cable ripper* for stripping plastic cable sheathing and insulation—fill out this list.

Plumbing Repair Tools

Screwdrivers come in handy for plumbing work, too. So do *rib-joint pliers* and the specialized wrenches mentioned below.

You'll need an *adjustable-end wrench* to loosen or tighten a variety of couplings, a *seat wrench* to remove worn faucet seats, an *allen wrench* to remove certain types of faucet handles, a *basin wrench* for hard to reach faucet nuts, and a *pipe wrench* to work with lengths of threaded pipe.

To renew worn faucet stem valve seats, get a *seat cutter*. To deal with stop-ups in drain lines, you can't afford to be without a *plunger* and a spring-steel *drain auger*.

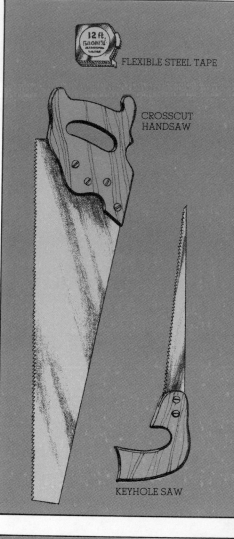

FLEXIBLE STEEL TAPE

CROSSCUT HANDSAW

KEYHOLE SAW

LONG-NOSE PLIERS

LINEMAN'S PLIERS

CONTINUITY TESTER

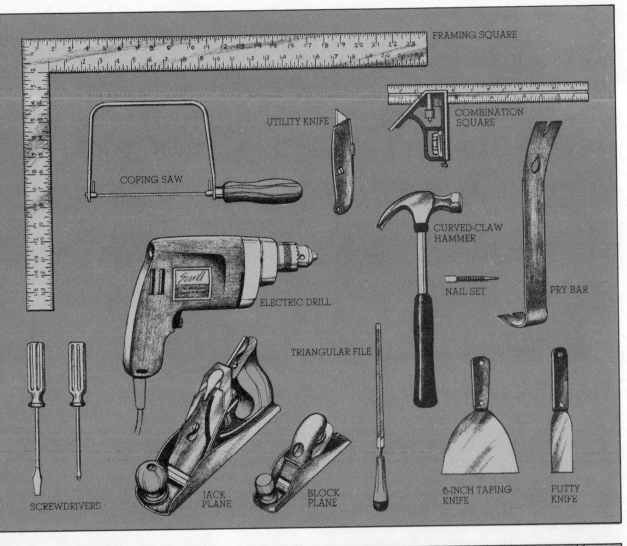

FRAMING SQUARE

UTILITY KNIFE

COMBINATION SQUARE

COPING SAW

CURVED-CLAW HAMMER

NAIL SET

PRY BAR

ELECTRIC DRILL

TRIANGULAR FILE

SCREWDRIVERS

JACK PLANE

BLOCK PLANE

6-INCH TAPING KNIFE

PUTTY KNIFE

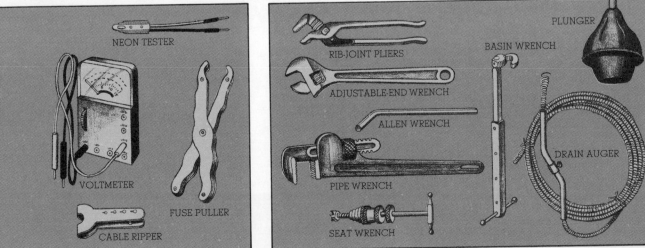

NEON TESTER

RIB-JOINT PLIERS

PLUNGER

BASIN WRENCH

VOLTMETER

ADJUSTABLE-END WRENCH

ALLEN WRENCH

DRAIN AUGER

FUSE PULLER

PIPE WRENCH

CABLE RIPPER

SEAT WRENCH

WALLS AND CEILINGS

If you'll look around with a critical eye at the walls and ceilings of your house, you'll be likely to spot at least a few surfaces in need of a face-lift. Maybe your problems are as minor as nail holes left behind after a mirror or some pictures were relocated, or as intimidating as a sagging lath-and-plaster ceiling. No matter what problems you find via your visual inspection, the next 10 pages of this book will leave you with no more excuses for letting them remain unfixed.

As you will find out on the following three pages, refurbishing drywall and plaster surfaces isn't nearly as demanding as

you may have thought. We take you step by step through the nuances of patching cracks, blemishes, and small and large holes in both drywall and lath-and-plaster surfaces. Then, because the repair must be made to blend in with the surrounding area, we show you how to re-texture the surface so professionally that only you will know where the problem used to be.

Concluding this section are how-to instructions for replacing moldings and for repairing damaged ceiling or wall tiles.

Repairing Drywall Surfaces

Setting Popped Nails

1 When you spot a popped nail, drive a 1½-inch ring-shank nail about 1½ inches above it, pressing in on the drywall panel as you do. Then create a "dimple" with your last hammer blow to set the nail just below the surface (but don't break through the drywall's thick paper facing). Now either remove the popped nail or sink it well into the surface with a nail set.

2 Fill the dimple and the old nail hole with joint compound, feathering it into the surrounding surface with a taping knife. Apply as many coats as necessary to make the surface smooth. Let the compound dry between coats. Finish and re-texture the repair following the instructions on page 12.

Mending Cracks and Bubbled Tape

1 You can repair minor cracks simply by filling the voids with compound. But if the joint tape curls up from the drywall surface, first use a utility knife to remove all loose tape. Be careful you don't remove the sound-fitting tape.

2 Cut a piece of joint tape to fit. Apply a bed of joint compound to the wall or ceiling, press the tape in place, and apply another coat of compound. Let dry, then add another layer of compound, then another if necessary. Feather each coat into the surrounding surface to help hide the seam. When the surface is smooth, finish the repair as instructed on page 12. *(continued)*

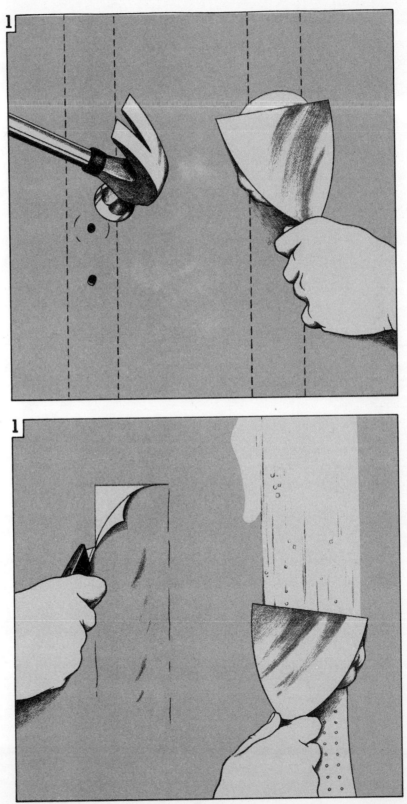

Patching Small Holes

1 Filling nail-size holes rates by far as the easiest drywall repair you can make. Use a putty knife to fill the hole with spackling compound, allowing some excess to "mound" above the surface. When the compound dries, lightly sand away the excess to leave a smooth surface.

An even easier procedure, although it is somewhat unorthodox, is to dispense with the spackling compound and the sanding, and simply fill small holes with white toothpaste. Believe it or not, it really works.

Patching Medium-Size Holes

1 Mending medium-size holes requires that you provide backing to which the joint compound can adhere. Fashion this backing from a scrap of perforated hardboard cut slightly larger than the hole, but small enough that you can maneuver it through the wall. To hold the scrap firmly against the back side of the wall, run a length of thin wire through a couple of the perforations as shown. Now, using joint compound, butter the perimeter of the backing as shown.

2 Insert the hardboard backing into the hole and center it behind

the opening. When dry, the joint compound will help the backing cling to the back of the drywall. To hold the backing in place during the interim, bridge the opening with a pencil and twist the wire ends together until the wire is taut. When the compound dries, clip the wire and remove it.

3 Now it's simply a matter of filling the recess with joint compound. Because the compound shrinks as it dries, you'll have to apply several coats to achieve satisfactory results. Let each coat dry before adding the next. Once you've completely filled in the void and don't see any

hairline cracks in the compound, sand the patch lightly and retexture its surface, following the instructions on page 12.

If you don't have any perforated hardboard around the house, try this alternative which uses a scrap of $1/4$- or $1/2$-inch plywood. Cut the plywood backing as you would the hardboard. Drill two holes in the center of the piece to run the wire through. Now follow through with the remaining steps as they are described above.

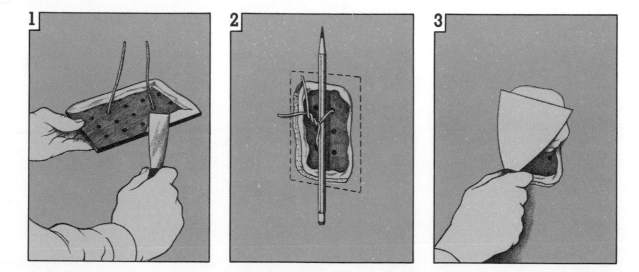

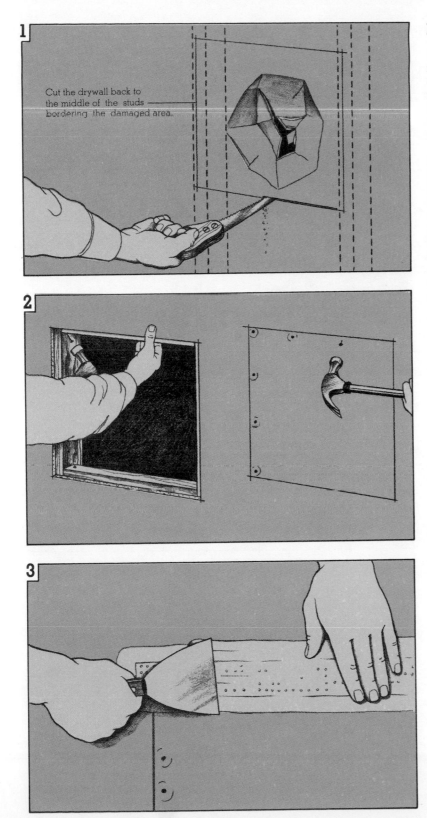

Cut the drywall back to the middle of the studs bordering the damaged area.

Patching Large Holes

1 After squaring off the area to be repaired, cut and remove the damaged drywall. Use a keyhole saw to make the horizontal cuts between the studs, and a sharp utility knife guided by a straightedge for the vertical cuts along the stud centers.

2 Fashion a like-size drywall patch from scrap drywall. Then cut two lengths of 2x2 to serve as backing supports for the top and bottom edges of the patch. Toenail the 2x2s in place, making sure they're flush with the edge of the studs. (Make this installation easier by first drilling angled starter holes for the nails.) Now fit the drywall patch into the opening and secure it with 1½-inch drywall nails spaced at least ⅜ inch in from the edges. "Dimple" each nailhead.

3 Lay down a bed coat of joint compound around the perimeter of the patch with a 4-inch taping knife held at a 45-degree angle to the wall. Avoid creating too much of a mound. Immediately center an appropriate length of drywall tape over each seam, using your hands to press it in place. Then with the taping knife, embed the tape further into the bed coat, holding one end of the tape secure with your other hand. Follow this with one or more coats of compound, feathering each coat into the surrounding surface and letting it dry thoroughly before applying the next. When the last coat has dried, finish and retexture the patch, following the steps on page 12. *(continued)*

Finishing and Retexturing the Surface

1 With enough care and patience, you can finish your drywall repairs so they'll be all but invisible.

Begin by smoothing the surface of the repair with either 80- or 100-grit coated abrasive or dampened sponge. (If you use an abrasive and the repair requires lots of sanding, be sure you wear a painter's mask to avoid inhaling too much gypsum dust. Also be careful not to sand all the way through the compound and into the tape. After sanding the area, wipe the dust off the surface with a dust cloth.)

2 Most drywall surfaces are not glassy smooth. Instead, they have a texture designed to conceal seams, nails, and minor defects in the drywall surface. You can closely duplicate most textures, each in a slightly different way. (It is a good idea to practice on a piece of scrap drywall before attempting to retexture the actual patch.)

You can approximate an "orange peel" texture by watering down some premixed joint compound and dabbing it over your repair with a sponge.

To blend a patch into a sand-textured surface, roll on some texture paint with a carpet-napped paint roller cover. To match an existing texture, apply a layer of drywall compound. Then, using a whisk broom or other stiff-bristled brush, replicate the pattern. If you're dealing with a travertine finish like the one shown, apply one layer of compound and let it set up slightly. Then, flick more compound onto the surface by using a paintbrush and knock off the high spots by lightly troweling the surface.

Beaded polystyrene and vermiculite textures on ceilings are hard to match. Although you can rent texturing equipment, your best solution may be to call in professional help to identify the type of finish you have and to duplicate its coarseness.

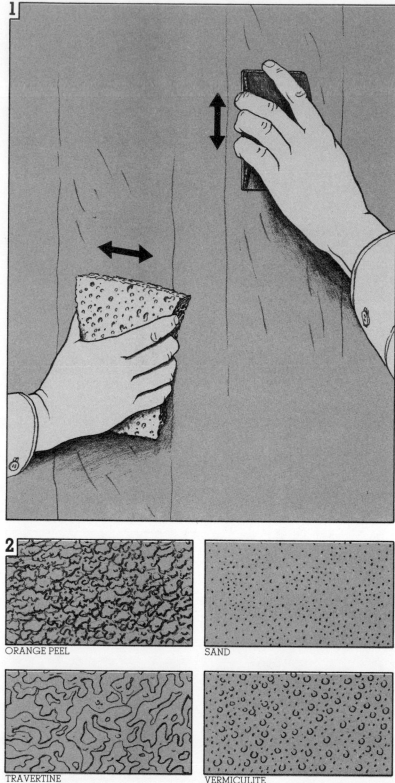

ORANGE PEEL

SAND

TRAVERTINE

VERMICULITE

Repairing Cracks and Holes in Plaster

Professional plasterers are scarce these days, but fortunately, with a little practice, you can handle most common plaster repairs yourself. Choose premixed spackling compound for small repairs such as hairline cracks and nail holes. For larger cracks and holes, however, mix powdered patching plaster with water—it's stronger than spackling compound and less prone to shrink.

Make plaster-patching a regular part of your prep work whenever you repaint. And be sure to correct any moisture leaks that might be responsible for your problems.

1 To prepare hairline cracks for patching, widen the fissures to about ⅛ inch with a screwdriver, then blow out any dust and debris that remain.

A hammer and cold chisel make short work of removing loose plaster from holes. To ensure a successful repair, work out in all directions until you reach sound plaster. Also knock the plaster from between the laths and undercut the edges as shown in the detail to help lock in the patching material.

2 If moisture has rotted the laths behind the loose plaster, cut the plaster back to at least the center of the studs adjacent to the damaged area. Remove the laths (if using a circular saw, adjust the blade to the proper depth) and nail up new wood or metal mesh-type laths.

3 To prevent the water in the plaster patching material from being drawn into surrounding surfaces and thereby weakening the patch, moisten the area shortly before making repairs. You can do this with either a spray bottle or a damp sponge. *(continued)*

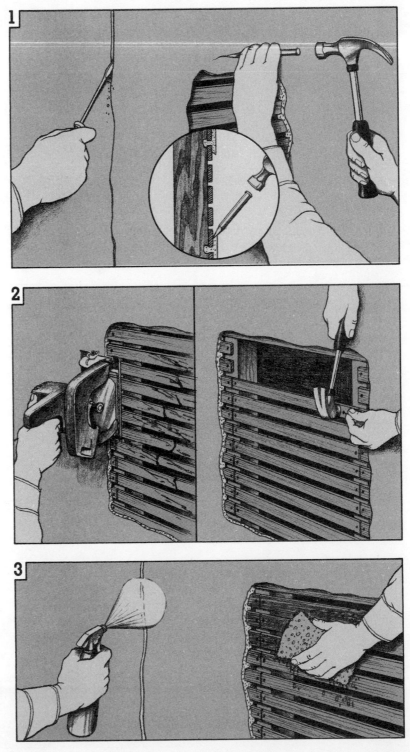

Repairing Cracks and Holes *(continued)*

4 Fill in hairline cracks by forcing spackling compound into the void with a putty knife. Let the compound dry, then apply another coat, if necessary, to bring the filler material flush with the surrounding surface.

When dealing with larger repairs, mix a batch of patching plaster according to the manufacturer's directions (on the package). Starting at the edges and using a 6-inch-wide taping knife, work the plaster into the undercuts, then fill in the center. (Make sure you apply enough pressure to the patch material so that some of it fills the spaces between the laths. This is known as *keying* [or tying] the plaster to its backing.)

Because patching plaster shrinks as it dries, be prepared to lay on two or more coats of material. Let each coat dry completely before applying the next. To achieve the best possible bond between coats, wet the surface of each base coat before laying on more plaster.

5 After the top coat of plaster has had sufficient drying time (at least 24 hours), it is ready for sanding. Using a medium-grade abrasive (80- or 100-grit) wrapped around a sanding block, sand the surface with light circular strokes. Focus a portable work light on the repair area to help detect slight surface irregularities you might otherwise overlook.

6 Never try to paint a plaster repair without first priming it. If you do, the new plaster will absorb paint more readily than the surrounding surface and your patch will show through.

Before you begin priming, however, make sure your new plaster has had sufficient time to cure and set up. To be safe, wait another 24 hours after you finish sanding.

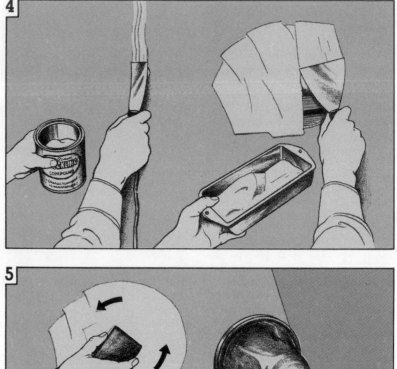

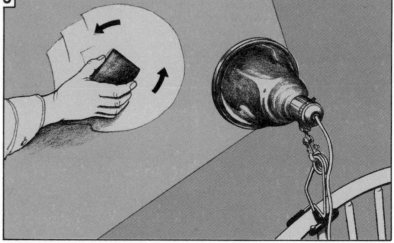

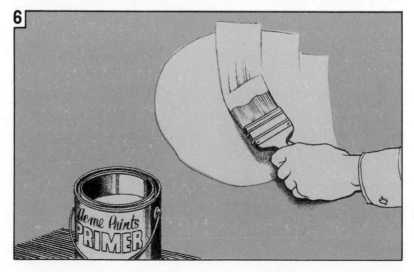

Replacing Damaged Moldings

Moldings, especially baseboard, base shoe, and door casing, take quite a beating in some homes. Perhaps you have accidentally broken a length of molding while trying to remove it. Maybe temperature and humidity changes in your home have dried out some of the moldings and caused them to split. Whatever the reason for undertaking a molding repair, you'll be relieved to know you're dealing with a relatively quick and easy task in most instances.

Finding an exact replacement for your damaged molding could very well turn out to be the hardest part of the job. Most lumberyards and home centers stock many of the popular molding profiles, but if you can't find one that matches what you have, seek out a supplier who can mill moldings to your specifications. (With older-style moldings this is often your only alternative.)

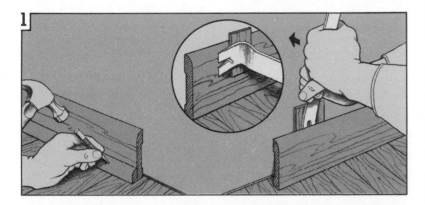

1 To remove a section of base shoe, first drive all finish nails deep within or through the molding. A nail set performs this task best. Then use a pry bar to work the molding up from the floor and away from the wall. Work carefully so you don't snap the molding.

To remove other types of molding, maneuver a pry bar behind the molding, using a wood scrap to protect the wall. Apply enough leverage to loosen the finish nails that hold the molding in place. Force the molding back against the wall. If the nailheads appear, pull them with the pry bar. If not, apply more leverage against the back side of the molding and pull the molding loose. Remove any nails that remain as shown in the detail.

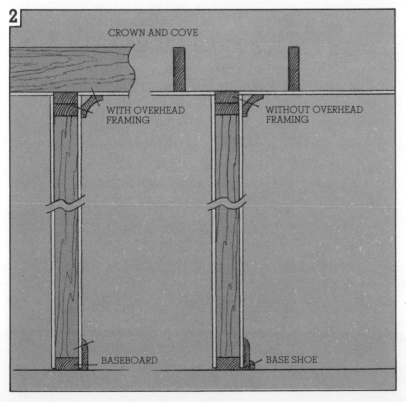

CROWN AND COVE

WITH OVERHEAD FRAMING

WITHOUT OVERHEAD FRAMING

BASEBOARD

BASE SHOE

2 When preparing to cut a replacement molding to size, lay the new piece over the old to get an accurate measurement. When cutting the replacement to fit, place crown and cove moldings in the miter box upside down; for all others, match the position the molding will take when in place.

Stain or paint your cut-to-size molding before you install it. Then attach it to your wall's framing members as shown with appropriately sized finish nails (don't nail only to plaster or drywall). You may need an inexpensive stud finder to locate studs behind your wall. Finish by setting the nailheads and filling the voids by thumbing in putty.

Replacing Damaged Ceramic and Plastic Wall Tiles

Normally, ceramic and plastic wall tiles stand up remarkably well for long periods. But sometimes one comes unglued or gets bumped and breaks. Occasionally you have to remove one or more tiles to correct another problem such as a leaky tub/shower valve.

Regluing a loose tile is the simplest of these situations to handle. Just purchase the adhesive designed for this job, apply some of it to the tile with a notched trowel, and press the tile into place. Regrout the joints as suggested in caption 4.

For help with the other two situations cited above, refer to the text and sketches that follow. (Note: If you don't have replacement tiles on hand, take a sample to your local tile dealer and hope you can find a close match.)

1 To replace a cracked tile, first remove the surrounding grout using an old screwdriver. For plastic tiles grouted with elastic joint filler, use a razor blade. Be careful not to chip or mar adjacent tiles.

2 Free the tile by prying it loose with a screwdriver inserted into a hole you've drilled with a carbide-tipped bit. If that fails, use a hammer and cold chisel. Then scrape or chip off (or remove chemically) the old adhesive and grout.

3 If a replacement ceramic tile must be cut, a glass cutter and straightedge work well. To trim tiles to irregular shapes, score the surface, then make the break with tile nippers or pliers. A coping saw works best for cutting plastic tiles.

To affix the new tile, spread adhesive on its back with a serrated trowel and press the tile in place.

4 Force grout into the joint spaces with a sponge or a rubber-faced trowel, and after 10 to 15 minutes, tool the joints with a rounded toothbrush handle or a moistened finger. Scrub off excess grout with a wet sponge, repeatedly rinsing it and wringing it out.

To grout plastic tiles, squeeze elastic filler into the joints, then smooth it with your finger.

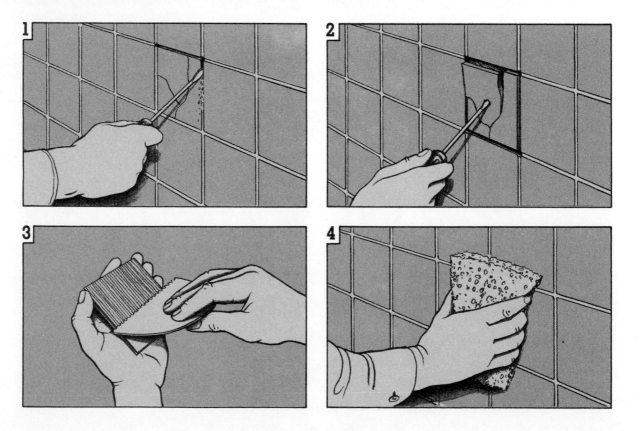

Repairing Damaged Ceiling Tiles

If you're stuck with dingy or water-damaged tiles overhead, apply a primer or clear sealer over the entire surface, then roll on new interior latex paint. (Note: Painting the tiles will reduce the sound absorbency of the ceiling.)

Dented tiles, however, should be replaced. Take a sample tile with you when you shop for replacements.

1 To remove a damaged tile, slice along its edges with a utility knife to cut through the flanges holding it in place. You may have to exert slight downward pressure with a pry bar or other tool to pop the tile free (see the detail). After removing the tile, pull out any remaining staples, tile material, or adhesive.

2 To insert a new tile, first cut off the tongue from one of its edges using a utility knife guided by a firmly held straightedge.

3 After you've applied panel adhesive to the furring strips, fit the tile into the groove of an adjacent tile. Press it flush with adjacent tiles and hold it until the adhesive has had a chance to set, or hold it with finish nails in each corner.

4 When replacing several adjoining tiles, secure most of them to the furring strips by stapling through the flanges of the tiles. (Read over steps 1 through 3 in order to place the last tile.)

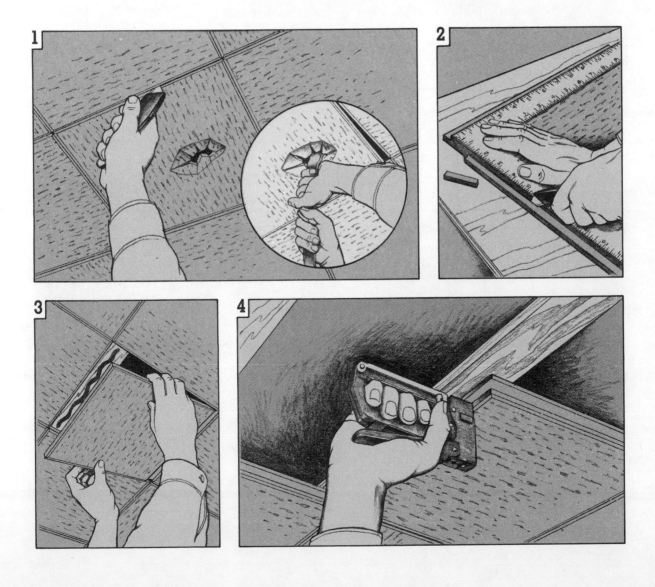

FLOORS AND STAIRS

When you stop to consider all of the weight and traffic borne by floors and stairs, it's really not surprising that they develop occasional problems that need attention. A stair tread can loosen and acquire an annoying squeak, and wood floors can become furniture-scuffed and need spot refinishing. Not even a tile floor is immune to accidents and the ordinary wear and tear that can leave you with tiles that need replacement.

This section may surprise you by pointing out the number of these jobs you can do yourself. On the next 11 pages we show you how to silence squeaks in wood floors and stairs, as well as how to touch up blemishes and replace damaged floorboards or parquet tiles. Those of you with resilient flooring, carpeting, or hard-surface materials underfoot will find help, too. We cover everything from removing stains to patching damaged areas. And where appropriate, we talk diagnosing the problem before launching into the repair steps involved. On top of this you also will find out what common household tools best suit the job at hand.

Silencing Floor and Stair Squeaks

Every house has at least one: a floorboard or stair tread that groans and creaks every time it's stepped on—and always the loudest when you go to make a midnight raid on the refrigerator.

Quieting those annoying squeaks is mainly a matter of locating them, then securing boards or stair components that have loosened and are rubbing against each other. If you're lucky, you'll have access to these trouble spots from below. If not, don't worry; we'll show you how to tackle them from above, too.

Silencing Floors From Above

1 With hardwood floors, drill angled pilot holes wherever needed, then drive spiral-shanked flooring nails into the subflooring. Set the nailheads and fill the recesses with color-matched wood putty.

2 For carpeted floors, pull back the carpeting and pad, then drive ring-shank nails into the floor joists beneath the squeaky floor.

Silencing Stairs From Above

1 To fasten down the front edges of a tread, drive spiral-shanked flooring nails at an angle into predrilled holes as shown. If you can round up a helper, have him or her stand on the tread as you nail. Next, set the nails and conceal the holes with wood putty.

To eliminate squeaks at the back edge of a tread, drive one or more wedges of scrap wood (coated with glue) into the gap between the treads and risers. Later, trim away the protruding wood.

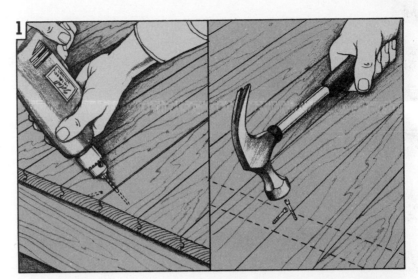

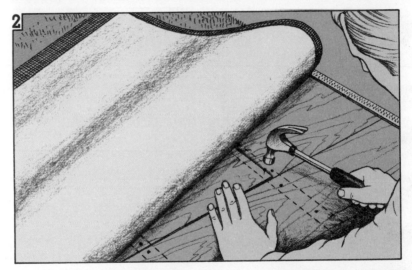

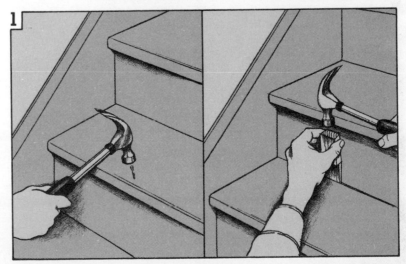

Silencing Floors From Below

1 Enlist a helper to walk on the finished floor above while you look for movement of the floor joists and of the subfloor from below. When you locate the problem area, first check to make sure that diagonal bridging between your floor joists (if any is nearby) is firm. Snugging it up may solve the problem.

If the noise comes from between the joists, drive a tight-fitting piece of solid bridging up between the joists until it makes contact with the subfloor, then end-nail it in place.

2 To silence a subfloor that has worked away from the joists, drive glue-coated shims into the gaps between the subfloor and the joists.

Silencing Stairs From Below

1 Squeaky stair treads that have parted company with their risers respond quite well to treatments from below.

First drill pilot holes through the small blocks of 2x2 for the wood screws that will attach to both the tread and the riser. Then coat the contacting surfaces of the blocks with wood glue and drive the screws in both directions.

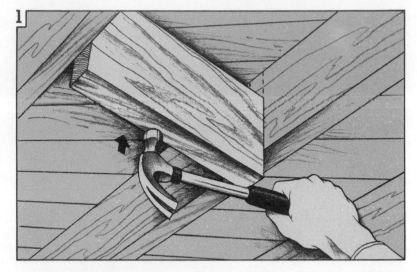

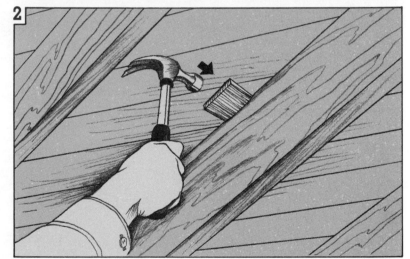

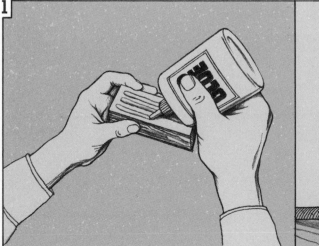

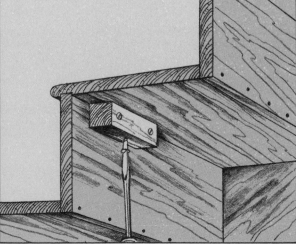

Other Wood Floor Repairs

On the previous two pages you learned how to silence your wood floors. Now we'll show you ways to restore their natural good looks—whether that involves smoothing away annoying scratches or replacing whole sections of damaged boards or tiles.

In both cases your success depends on how well you match your repair to the surrounding floor. So be sure to exercise all due care when removing the damaged flooring and when selecting stains and replacement boards or tiles. When purchasing new wood flooring, take a sample of what you have now so the salesperson can provide you with an exact match.

Hiding Scratches

1 To hide minor imperfections on waxed or varnished floors, first try rubbing the scratched areas with a rag moistened with stain that approximates the stain on your floor.

For surface cuts that don't "disappear" when you treat the surface with stains, use steel wool and a solvent such as cleaning fluid. Realize, however, that if you apply solvent, you'll need to rinse, then refinish, the treated area.

2 You can lift off most food stains and heel and caster marks by buffing the surface with the grain, using fine steel wool moistened with mineral spirits. This technique works especially well for oil-finished wood floors. With acrylic finishes, you'll also need to refinish the area you've abraded.

Replacing Damaged Wood Flooring

1 To remove one damaged floorboard, make several cuts down the center of the board with a circular saw. Adjust the cutting *(continued)*

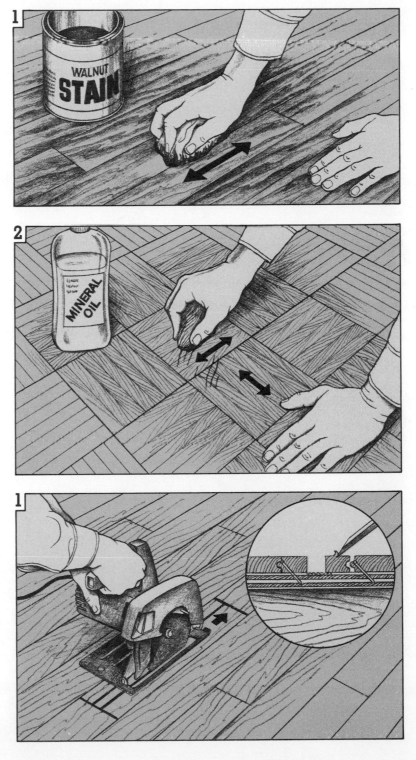

Replacing Damaged Wood Flooring *(Cont.)*

depth to the thickness of the flooring (usually ³/₈ to ³/₄ inch) so you won't damage the subfloor. Work from the center toward the ends to avoid overcutting.

Now chisel out the board, starting with the kerfed midsection and finishing with the sides. Be careful not to damage the groove of the adjacent board.

2 When you're dealing with more than one damaged board, begin by outlining the perimeter of the area to be replaced using a framing square. Go only as far as the edges of the nearest sound boards.

Now, with your circular saw adjusted to the proper cutting depth, cut along the ends of your outline (across the boards, not along their length). Again, cut from the center to the edges. Then make a series of cuts along the length of the damaged area, as was done for the single-board replacement described at the bottom of the previous page.

3 To remove the boards, wedge or drive a pry bar between a couple of the lengthwise cuts as shown, then work it back and forth until you're able to lift one of the boards. Continue prying boards loose one by one.

If you're working with parquet flooring, dispense with sawing and simply nibble away at individual tiles, relying on a hammer and wood chisel to do the job.

4 Secure replacement boards with finish nails blind-nailed through their tongues at about a 50-degree angle. To fit the last board, you'll have to chisel off the bottom of its groove, as shown. Now apply floor adhesive to the subfloor, to the tongue, and to the half-groove of the board, then tap it in place.

Glue replacement parquet tiles with wood tile floor adhesive.

Repairing Resilient Goods

Other than giving a resilient surface floor an occasional buffing with wax or vinyl brightener to help hide minor scratches and renew the original luster, most people assume there's not much a do-it-yourselfer can do with this type of flooring material if problems develop. Not true! Provided that you can lay your hands on matching tiles or sheet goods, you shouldn't have any major difficulties, procedurally, at least, replacing a damaged tile or section of sheet goods and making your floor look almost new again. (Note: The older and more worn the goods, the harder it will be to make the repair unobtrusive.)

Replacing Tiles

1 Begin by covering over the damaged tile with a dampened cloth. Now run a warm iron back and forth across the damaged tile to soften both the tile and the underlying adhesive. (Also use this technique when you simply need to dab more adhesive under a good tile whose corner has curled.)

If you don't have an iron handy, a propane torch works just as well. With this, however, take care that you do not scorch any of the surrounding tile.

2 Score the perimeter of the tile with a utility knife and straightedge. Then, using a stiff-bladed putty knife, pry up the softened tile. If this doesn't do the job, use a hammer and chisel, working out from the tile's center.

3 Scrape away the old tile adhesive and apply new adhesive with a notched trowel. *(continued)*

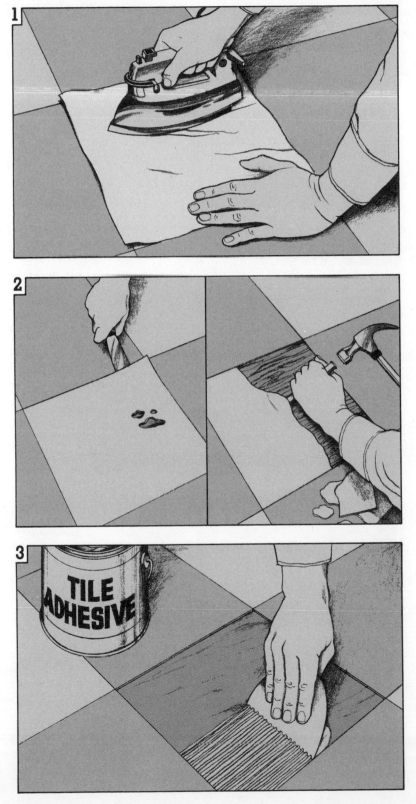

Replacing Tiles *(cont.)*

4 Before laying the replacement tile, warm it slightly under a damp cloth and iron to make it more flexible. Then align one edge with adjoining tile and press (don't slide) it in place.

Immediately clean up any excess adhesive and weight down the new tile with a heavy object.

Patching Sheet Goods

Repairing a damaged area in sheet flooring is essentially like replacing a damaged floor tile: You lay in a "tile patch" that you've cut from a piece of matching sheet goods. But unlike working with tiles, patching sheet goods demands a bit more attention to correctly sizing the patch and carefully matching its pattern to that of the existing floor.

1 Start by positioning the patch material over the damaged area, taking care to align it so the pattern matches the flooring exactly. Secure the patch to the floor with masking tape.

2 Cut through the overlay and the damaged flooring, using a utility knife guided by a straightedge. Make sure your cuts remain outside the damaged area. Cutting along pattern lines helps to conceal the patch.

Remove the old flooring just as if it were a tile (see the sketches opposite and above). Before you apply new adhesive for your patch, trial-fit the patch into the cleaned out opening. You may need to lightly sand the patch's edges for a perfect fit. Finish by placing a weight on the patch.

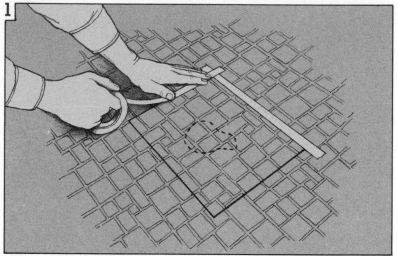

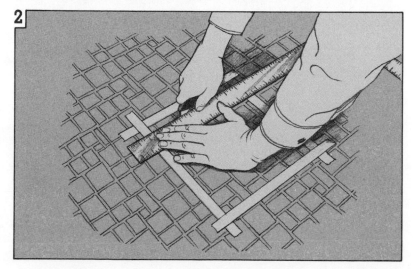

Carpeting Repairs

Removing Stains

Whatever the carpet stain, your first concern should be the same: Treat it as quickly as you can. To remove one of the stains listed in the chart at right, follow the suggested procedure. For other stains and for those you can't identify, use the technique described below.

With still-wet liquid stains, first blot the soiled area with a clean dry cloth. Then use a spoon to remove any solids you can, if there are any. Now treat the stain with dry-cleaning fluid, followed by a detergent-vinegar solution (1 teaspoon of each in a quart of warm water). Blot again, then let the area dry. If needed, reapply whichever cleaner seems to work best, dry again, and brush gently to restore the pile.

Replacing Damaged Sections

Don't attempt to patch-repair a section of carpeting that already shows noticeable wear: Your new-looking patch will probably stand out more than the original damage. Take care to install patches with the pile running in the same direction as the surrounding carpet. With rubber-backed (or other glued-down) carpet, simply glue in your cut-to-size patch. For jute-backed carpet installed with tack strips, follow these steps:

1 Start by piercing the carpet near a wall with an awl and pull the goods up off its tack strips until you have access to the back side of the damaged area. Jot down the exact dimensions of your outline. *(cont.)*

Treating Common Carpet Stains

Stain or Problem	Treatment	Notes
Wax, Grease, Tar, and Chewing Gum	Remove as much of the solid as you can by gently scraping with a dull knife or a spoon. Treat the stain with dry-cleaning fluid.	For chewing gum, apply ice cubes in a plastic bag to harden the gum before scraping.
Cigarette Burns	Snip off the darkened ends of carpet fibers and gently blot the area with a detergent-vinegar solution.	This procedure masks burn damage. For complete repair, patching is necessary.
Lipstick	Gently blot the stain with dry-cleaning fluid, then with detergent-vinegar solution. Rinse with a solution of 1 tablespoon of ammonia in a cup of water.	
Animal Stains, Fruit Juices	If the stain is still wet or fresh, repeatedly sponge it with lukewarm water. Blot dry and treat with detergent-vinegar solution. Wait 15 minutes, blot again, and sponge the area with clean water.	Stains that have caused your carpet to change color often cannot be removed.
Paint	Treat oil-based paints with turpentine, water-based paints with warm water.	
Ink	Treat ball point pen ink by blotting just the ink stain with denatured alcohol.	Permanent ink is just what its name implies. Minimize stain by blotting at once with water.

Replacing Damaged Sections *(continued)*

2 After using your framing square and a utility knife to cut out the damaged area, outline a patch of the same dimensions on the back side of your patch. Note the direction in which the patch's pile will need to run when laying out the outline, then cut the patch with a framing square and utility knife.

3 Lay the carpeting back down over the tack strips and carefully insert your patch (check pile direction). Make sure none of the carpet fibers gets folded over.

Now carefully fold back the carpeting, lay seam tape (adhesive side down) along the perimeter of the patch, and heat the tape with an iron until the adhesive melts. (Don't forget to clean your iron while it's still warm.)

4 Weight the taped seams with a heavy object to help ensure a good bond. Don't disturb the patch for at least 15 minutes.

5 To re-stretch the carpet and fasten it to the tack strips, you'll need a special carpet-laying tool called a *knee kicker*, which you can rent from any rental outlet.

Position the head of the kicker about ¾ inch from the wall and kick its butt end with your knee. Work from each end toward the corner of the room.

Mending Torn or Damaged Seams

Seam splits much longer than three feet or so are best repaired by a carpet layer. But short seams, such as the kind found in hallways, respond well to the do-it-yourself repair we explain here. This technique is intended for jute-backed carpet only. To mend

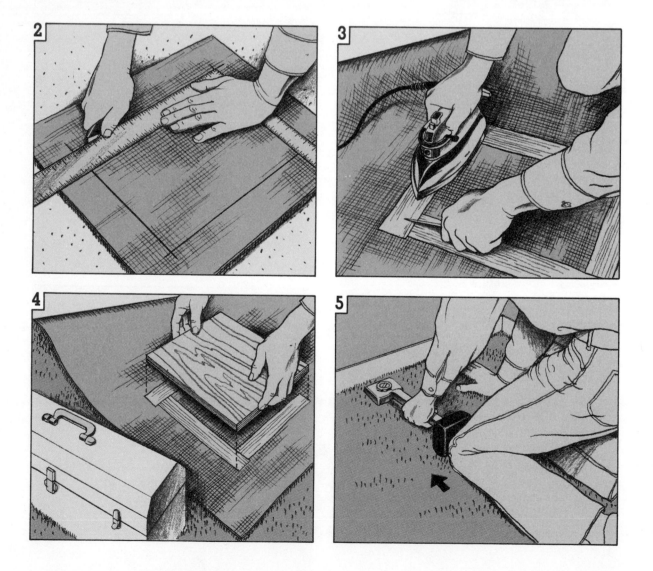

seams in rubber-backed goods or any other carpet that is glued to the floor, apply a bead of seam adhesive to both edges, join the pieces, and place a weight on them for several hours.

1 Split the seam along its entire length (be careful not to cut any carpet fibers) and roll back both pieces of carpet. Because new seam tape won't adhere to the old, remove the existing tape by softening its adhesive with a hot iron.

2 If necessary, stretch the carpet with a knee kicker so the edges of the two pieces meet but don't overlap. Secure the carpet in its correct position by driving a row of nails a short distance back from the seam line. Center new seam tape along the seam line (adhesive side up) and melt its adhesive with a hot iron. Lay both edges onto the tape, being careful not to overlap them. Weight the seam for 15 minutes.

Getting Rid of Bubbles

Carpet that is constantly exposed to moisture or that wasn't stretched tightly enough in the first place can develop bubbles. To get rid of these unsightly and potentially dangerous problem areas, use this tightening technique.

1 Pull the carpet (in the affected area) off its tack strips, and re-stretch it as shown in sketch 5 on page 26. (In large rooms you will need to rent a so-called *power stretcher* to apply adequate tension.) Once you've pulled the carpet tight, run a wide-blade chisel along the wall-floor line to crease the carpet and further push it onto the tack strips.

2 Trim the excess carpet slightly above the crease using a sharp utility knife.

3 Finally, use an awl to tuck the raw edge behind the tack strips.

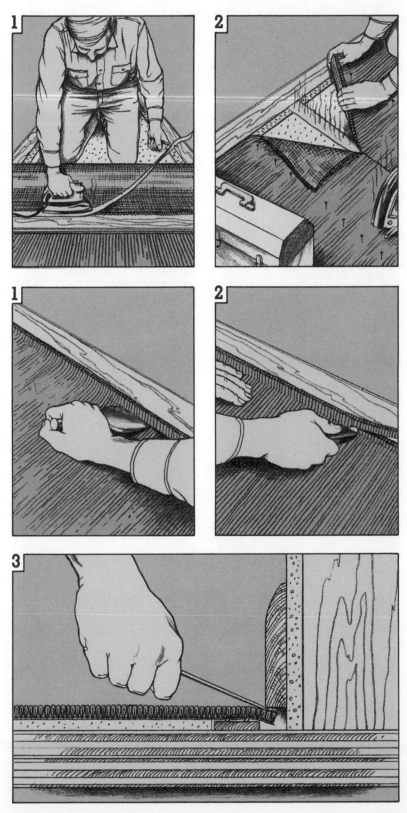

Hard-Surface Flooring Repairs

Part of the beauty of hard-surface floors like tile, brick, and slate is that they require little maintenance. But occasionally you'll still need to remove stains and (less frequently) patch a crack or replace a damaged tile. After reading this and the facing page, you'll have the know-how to handle any such problem you may encounter.

Removing Common Stains

Regardless of the type of stain you need to remove from your hard-surface floor, the sooner you do it, the better. Always wear rubber gloves when working with harsh chemicals, and never use flammable solvents around an open flame.

The chart at right lists cures for common stains on ceramic and quarry tiles, slate, and brick, as well as on grout and concrete. For stains of an unknown nature, consult a flooring dealer for advice.

Filling Cracks and Voids in Concrete

1 Prepare the damaged area by chipping away and brushing out all loose concrete. Then use a hammer and cold chisel to undercut its edges to "lock in" the patch.

2 Now fill the void with latex or epoxy patching material, packing it in with a taping knife or a rectangular trowel. Check the manufacturer's instructions on whether to dampen or otherwise treat the area before filling.

Treating Common Hard-Surface Flooring Stains

Material	Stain	Treatment
Ceramic Tile	Soap Film	Scrub with vinegar; rinse.
	Grease	Keep wet 1 hour with a 1:4 lye-water solution, then rinse and dry.
	Gum, Tar, Wax	Scrape off solids; treat remainder with a rag soaked in kerosene; dry.
	Inks, Dyes	Keep stain wet with household bleach. Warm-water rinse and dry.
	Food Stains	Scrub with trisodium phosphate solution (or bleach); rinse and dry.
	Paint	Soften and remove with acetone.
Brick Pavers, Concrete, Grout	Efflorescence	Scrub with a 1:15 (for light bricks) or 1:10 (for dark bricks) solution of muriatic acid and water. Let stand, then rinse. (Don't apply acids to colored concrete or grout.)
	Grease	Absorb what you can with sawdust or powdered cement, dissolve remaining with a degreaser. Lighten with bleach.
	Paint	For wet paint, use the appropriate solvent. For dried paint, use a remover.
	Rust	Scrub in bleach, let stand, then rinse.
	Soot	Scrub in scouring powder, then rinse.
Slate Quarry Tile		Blot all spills at once and scrub with detergent. Spills that penetrate these porous materials become permanent stains. To prevent stains, apply a sealer.

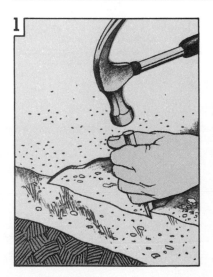

Replacing and Regrouting Tile

1 When a single tile in a field of hard-surface flooring is damaged and needs replacement, here is how to proceed. (To replace loose or deteriorated grout, omit steps 3 and 4.)

Begin by chipping out the old grout with a hammer and a cold chisel held at an angle. As you work, be careful not to damage sound adjacent tiles.

2 When all of the old grout has been loosened, clean out the joints surrounding the tile with a stiff-bristled whisk broom.

3 With the joint spaces cleaned, you now have room to chip away at the damaged tile. Using a hammer and cold chisel, begin chipping at the center of the tile and work toward the edges. Always wear eye protection when working with a cold chisel.

4 To set the replacement tile, use a notched trowel to apply adhesive evenly to the tile's back. (Ask your tile supplier which type of notched trowel—there are many—best suits the kind of adhesive and flooring you intend to use.) When overlaying a wood or resilient floor, use an epoxy cement. For concrete surfaces, dealers recommend thin-set mortar. Carefully center the tile and press (don't slide) it in place.

5 After the adhesive has had at least 24 hours to dry, fill the joint spaces with mortar, using a household sponge. You can add pigment to the new grout to match the existing joints if necessary. Wipe off the excess grout with a clean, dampened sponge.

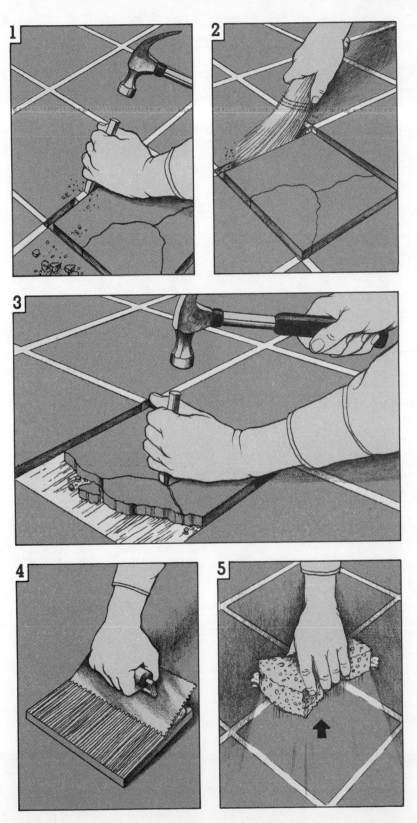

WINDOWS

Because we use windows to brighten the inside of our homes with sunshine and provide us with a view of our outdoor surroundings, we seldom notice them. But occasionally, when an errant baseball finds its way through a glass pane, or when a sash absolutely refuses to budge, or when a screen needs repairing or replacing, windows make their presence known. This chapter was written for those occasions.

Realize, however, that with proper maintenance you can do a great deal to prevent some window problems. To keep windowsills from rotting, for example, make sure they always have a protective coat of paint. Check them each spring and fall. To keep movable sashes working, periodically clean the channels they ride in. You'll be amazed at how smoothly you can make crank-operated windows perform with a squeeze of powdered graphite or a drop of penetrating oil in and around the crank mechanism periodically.

On the next 11 pages you'll find the solutions to a host of window problems, including damaged screening, broken panes, rotted sills, balky sashes, and many others. No longer will you have to go to the expense of hiring a repairman, or worse, ignore the repair completely.

Repairing Screening

Holes and tears in screens are among the most put-off repairs around most homes. That's probably because they're not as urgent as a leaky faucet or a binding door or some of the other must-do repair jobs. But you can only procrastinate so long because eventually you won't be able to get fresh air in the house without allowing a horde of pesky flies or mosquitoes in with it.

So if you have one or more screens in need of attention, there's no better time than now to take corrective action. On this and the next two pages, we show you how to repair both small tears and gaping holes in screening as well as how to replace screening in both wood and metal frames.

The tools and materials for screen work are, with a few exceptions, as common home workshop tools as you can find. For mending, you'll need silicone glue or tin snips and a small amount of aluminum or fiber glass. To replace a wood-framed screen, you'll need a putty knife, a screwdriver, a staple gun, some scrap wood strips for stretching the replacement screening, a hammer and brads, and a utility knife. For work on metal sashes, you also may need a length of replacement plastic spline. To make screening replacement work easier still, consider investing in a special screening tool.

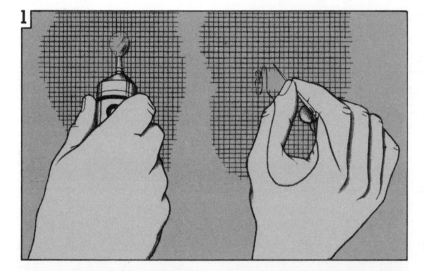

Mending Small Holes

1 Very small tears in metal or fiberglass screening respond well to mending with clear silicone glue. If necessary, dab it on in successive layers until the tear is completely filled.

You can "darn" small holes in metal screening. Unravel a strand or two from a piece of scrap screening and sew the hole shut, weaving the strands into the sound fabric with a needle.

Patching Large Holes

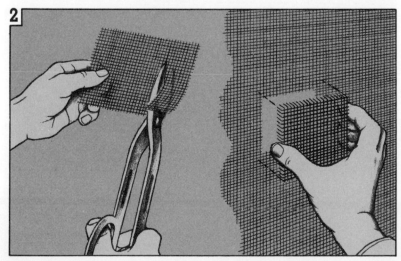

2 To repair large holes in metal screening, start by neatly trimming the damage to a ravel-free square or rectangle using tin snips. Now cut a piece of patch screening that is about two inches larger (overall) than the damaged area.

Unravel a couple of the patch's strands on each side and bend them over at a 90-degree angle. Position the patch over the opening and thread the bent wires through the sound fabric. Then bend the wires over to hold the patch in place.

The technique is even simpler for fiber-glass screening. Cut a patch of similar material with scissors and affix it with transparent-silicone glue.

Replacing Wood-Framed Screening

1 To remove the damaged screening from the frame, pry up on the wood molding strips with a putty knife. Start with the frame's center rail, if it has one, and work from the centers of the strips to their edges. Now remove all of the staples you have exposed and lift out the screening.

To cut your replacement screening to the correct size, unroll a length of it and cut a piece that is several inches wider and at least a foot longer than the frame. Fold over the top edge of the screening about ½ inch and staple this hemmed double layer as shown here, working from the center to the edges.

2 Before stapling the remaining edges of the screening in place, you'll need to make an improvised "stretcher" from a pair of 1x2s. Nail the bottom 1x2 to the floor or a bench, then position the bottom of the frame an inch or two away from the 1x2, with the excess screen lying over it. Now nail the second 1x2 atop the first so the screening is sandwiched between them.

3 Insert two wedges (made by cutting a 1x4 diagonally) between the 1x2 cleats and the bottom of the frame. Now tap the wedges with a hammer until the screening becomes taut. (Tap the wedges gently, alternating sides and being careful to avoid overstretching the screening.)

4 Now staple the bottom edge in place, followed by the sides (pull on the fabric to tighten it before stapling), and finally the center rail, if there is one. Again, begin stapling at the centers, and smooth the mesh as you work out toward the edges.

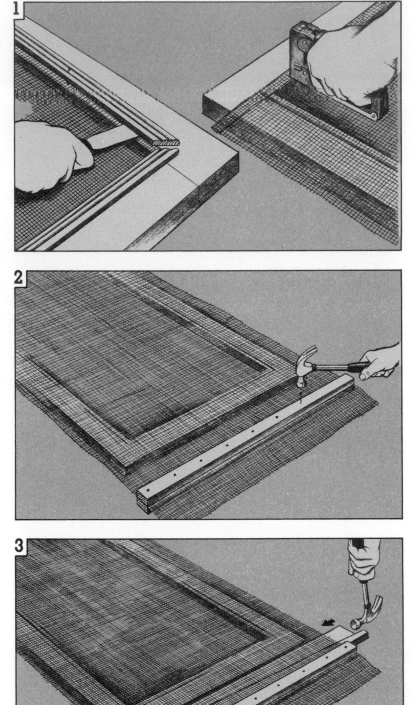

Finish the installation by trimming away the excess from the frame sides and bottom with a utility knife. Refit the screen molding with countersunk brads. Fill the recesses with wood filler.

Replacing Metal-Framed Screening

1 Unlike screens in wood frames, metal-framed screens are held in place by a spline that's friction-fit into a channel around the perimeter of the frame. Removing a damaged screen is simply a matter of prying loose this spline with the blade of a screwdriver.

2 Cut your replacement screen to the same size as the frame's outer dimensions, trimming the corners at 45-degree angles (to make them easier to tuck in). Now use a putty knife to bend an edge of the screen into the channel along one side.

3 Secure this edge by driving a spline (the original or a replacement) into the channel with a hammer and wooden block. Have a helper pull the opposite edges taut, then pull the other two taut as you tap in the remaining splines. Trim away the excess screening with a utility knife. Note in the detail the special screening tool that makes this task even easier.

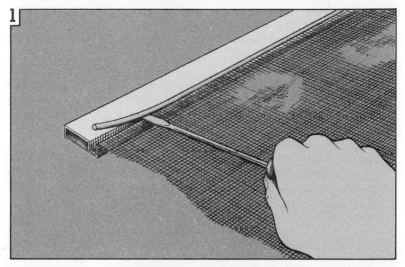

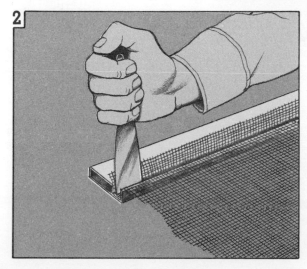

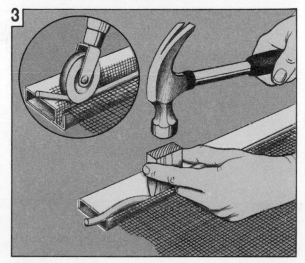

Replacing Broken Windows

Expect to pay dearly if a repairman comes to your house to replace a broken window. Most won't even take on small jobs such as this, and the few who do are forced to charge what may appear to be an exorbitant amount. All the more reason to do the job yourself. The techniques for repairing wood- and metal-framed sashes differ considerably, but neither is difficult. Just be sure to wear heavy gloves whenever you work with glass panes.

Reglazing Wood-Framed Windows

1 Start by removing any loose shards of broken glass, then use an old wood chisel to pry up the glazing compound that holds the pane in place. (Soften the compound with a propane torch if necessary.) Remove the old glazier's points which hold the pane in place.

2 Determine the size replacement pane needed by measuring the cleaned-out opening. Subtract 1/16 inch from each dimension (1/8 inch for acrylic panes).

3 Have a glass supplier cut your replacement pane to size or cut your own. To cut your own, make a single score along each cutoff line with a glass cutter guided by a framing square.
   Then place the score over the dowel or the edge of a table and snap off the scrap piece. Trim any rough edges with pliers.

4 Prime the rabbetted area of the frame in which the pane will rest with linseed oil, wait 20 minutes, then lay on a 1/16-inch bed coat of glazing compound.

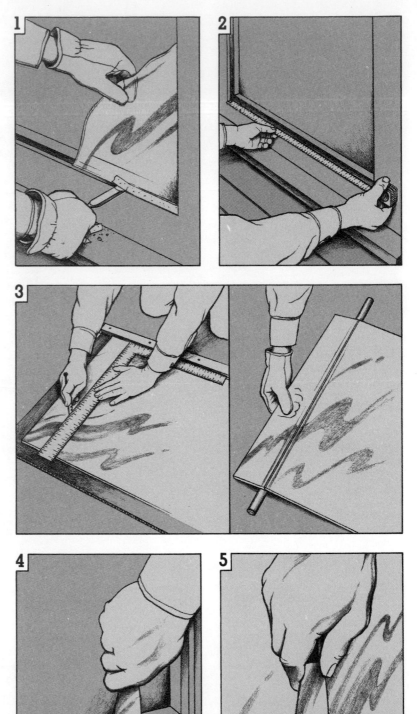

5 Position the glass pane, insert matchsticks around the perimeter to center the glass in the opening, and press into the glazing compound. Install two metal glazier's points per side as shown.

6 To complete the installation, roll some glazing compound into a ¼-inch "rope" and press it around the sash edges.

7 Bevel the compound with a putty knife held at a 30- to 40-degree angle. Allow a week for the compound to dry, then paint around the installation, overlapping the glass about ¹⁄₁₆ inch for a tight weather seal. Don't clean the window until the paint has dried.

Reglazing Metal-Framed Windows

1 Metal sashes come in a variety of configurations. Some are of one-piece construction in which glass is held in place by removable metal clips (augmented by glazing compound) or a flexible spline. Other sashes, the kind glaziers refer to as "knock-aparts," have frames that disassemble for reglazing. With the exception of some of the one-piece spring-clip types, you should remove all metal sashes from their frames when working on them.

Like wood sashes, the *one-piece steel sashes* (the kind often found in basement windows) hold glass in place with glazing compound. But underneath it, metal spring clips take the place of glazier's points. *One-piece aluminum frames* use a vinyl or rubber spline, which you can pry out with a screwdriver and re-install with a putty knife.

In the *"knock-apart"* category, many sliding sashes are held together with edge-driven screws at their corners. Once removed, you simply pull the frame members away from the glass. Some pin-type aluminum frames have internal L-brackets "dimpled" in place at their corners. To release them, drill out the dimples. To reassemble, make new dimples with an awl to hold the L-bracket in place.

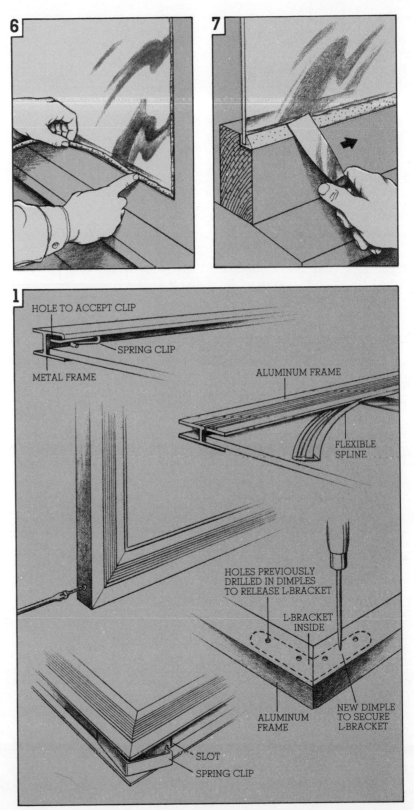

HOLE TO ACCEPT CLIP · SPRING CLIP · METAL FRAME · ALUMINUM FRAME · FLEXIBLE SPLINE · HOLES PREVIOUSLY DRILLED IN DIMPLES TO RELEASE L-BRACKET · L-BRACKET INSIDE · ALUMINUM FRAME · NEW DIMPLE TO SECURE L-BRACKET · SLOT · SPRING CLIP

Replacing Rotted Windowsills

Considering the soaking they get in wet weather and the baking they get when the sun shines, it's no wonder windowsills need a little more maintenance than most other household components.

The best way to keep your windowsills dry and free of rot is an annual treatment that includes puttying cracks, caulking, and repainting. To save a problem sill that has a few cracks and voids, scrape it clean and soak it with a wood preservative such as pentachlorophenol. Wait a day, then soak it again with boiled linseed oil. Finally, putty all cracks, prime, and repaint.

If you're stuck with a sill that's barely hanging in there, resign yourself to replacing it, following the steps.

1 As this cutaway of a typical double-hung window shows, a sill is surrounded by an interlocking assortment of trim and framing components, both outside the window and inside. To get at the sill, you need to remove the *apron* and *stool* moldings. (Pry these away very carefully so you'll be able to reuse them.)

2 Rather than attempt to remove the old sill in one piece, use a handsaw to cut completely through it adjacent to each jamb. Be careful not to cut into the exterior siding. You should now be able to lift the large center section directly up and out (save it for use as a sample when you buy a replacement sill). Using a hammer and, if necessary, a chisel, drive the remaining sill material out from under the side jambs. The wood should split into easy-to-remove chunks.

3 After you've cut your replacement sill to size, soak it with a wood preservative. When it's ready to install, gently tap it in place with a hammer and wooden block. If the sill doesn't fit the first time, don't force it. Instead, drive it back out, lightly sand the areas under the jambs, and try again.

4 To ensure that the sill sits tightly against the jambs, you may need to drive in wood shims as shown. When you have a snug fit, drive galvanized finish or casing nails through the sill and into the shims and framing underneath. Snap off or saw through the excess shim material. Sink and fill the nailheads, and caulk around the sill to fill any gaps. Prime and paint the new sill, then reposition the apron and stool moldings.

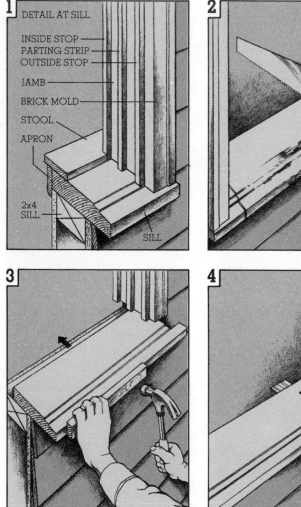

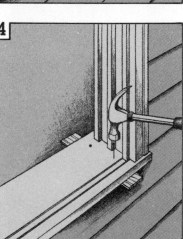

Repairing Double-Hung Windows

Freeing a Balky Sash

Few things can make you feel more helpless, not to mention more frustrated, than trying to raise or lower a window sash that refuses to cooperate. Below we show and discuss several strategies that should help you free up that bind and keep your blood pressure at a manageable level.

1 If your sash barely moves, dirt may have accumulated in its channels. Try cleaning the channels, then lubricating them with a bar of soap or a paraffin block.

2 If a sash won't move at all, and you haven't used the window since you painted last, the paint may have sealed it shut. To break such a seal, first try wedging an old broad-bladed putty knife between the sash and the stops adjoining it. Gently tap the knife with a hammer, then work it back and forth. Do this along the entire length of the sash and on both sides.

3 No luck? Then grab a pry bar. Working from the outside of the house, force the bar between the sill and the bottom rail and apply upward pressure. Repeat this procedure at several different points along the sill if necessary.

4 To free a sash that has swollen because of moisture, you have a couple of options. You can drive a block of wood that's about 1/16 inch wider than the sash channel up and down the channel to "spread" the stops enough to allow free movement of the sash. If this doesn't get things moving, sand the base of each of the sash channels as well as the inside edges of the stops to provide a bit more clearance for the sash.

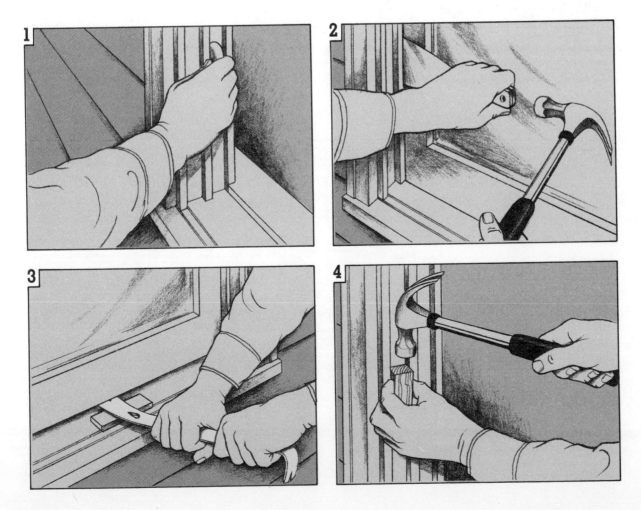

Replacing Sash Cords

Many double-hung windows are outfitted with a set of counterbalances that allow you to open the window to any height. Some manufacturers use a pair of *sash weights* and *sash cords* on each side of the window as the lifting mechanism. Others you'll see use *spring/spiral balances* to accomplish the same end (see the facing page). As long as proper balance is maintained, the window will work. But as with anything mechanical, adjustment is sometimes needed.

If your windows are the sash cord and weight type like the one shown here, and if they just stay open or cause other trouble, you can bet that one or more sash cords have broken. Here's how to solve that problem quickly.

1 Pry the inside stop molding away from the frame in several spots with a wide-bladed putty knife. (Replace an upper-sash cord by removing the parting strip.)

2 To free the sash, lift it enough to clear the stool and swing it out.

3 Remove the sash cord from its keyed slot in the side of the sash.

4 Unscrew the access panel on the jamb and take out the sash weight.

5 Feed the replacement cord (or sash chain) over the pulley and watch for it to appear at the access panel. (This is also a good time to lubricate the pulley if needed.)

6 Tie the new cord to the sash weight, return the weight to its rightful place, and knot the free end to the sash, permitting the weight to hang three inches above the sill when the sash is fully raised (or the upper sash is lowered). Replace the window and all stops.

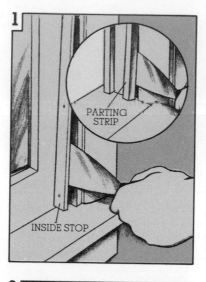

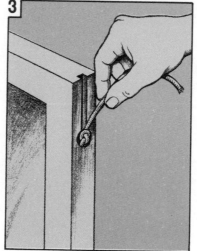

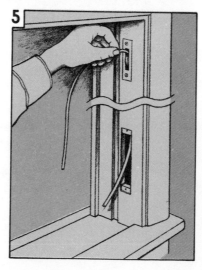

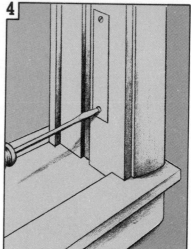

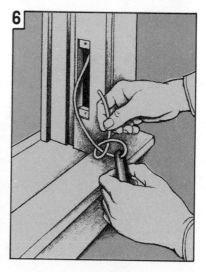

Fixing Spring/ Spiral Balances

Window-balance mechanisms with springs and spiral twist rods are relatively maintenance-free. When a problem occurs, it's usually because a window has remained closed for an extended period, leaving its spring in a stretched-out position and thus weakening it. As you'll see, restoring smooth operation is a simple adjustment. More rarely, a spring will rust or break, or the spiral twist rod will become bent. When that happens, it's easiest to replace the entire unit.

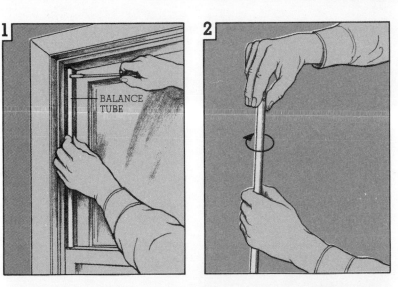

Adjusting Spring-Loaded Balances

1 To increase the tension of a window of this type, get a good grip on the spring-loaded balance tube and loosen the screw that holds it to the window frame.

2 Now rotate the tube in a clockwise direction three or four revolutions. Then reattach the tube with the screw. Repeat this procedure with the tube on the opposite side of the window.

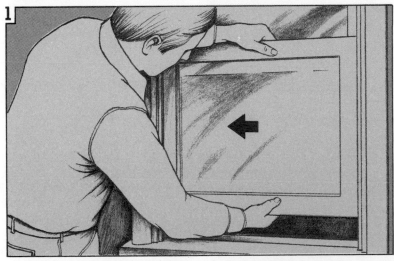

Replacing Spring-Loaded Balances

1 Start by removing the screw holding the spring balance mechanism in place, then allow the balance to unwind fully. Now force the sash to one side or the other (the channels the sashes ride in are spring-loaded to permit easy removal of the sash).

2 Using a pry bar, pry out the sash, being careful not to damage the woodwork.

3 Disengage the old mechanism by unscrewing the metal plate that attaches it to the bottom of the sash. After installing the new balance, replace the sash.

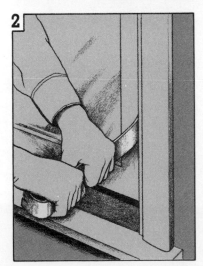

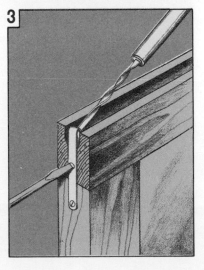

Repairing Crank-Operated Windows

The convenience of crank-operated casement, awning, and jalousie windows is a luxury akin to having power windows on your car. Unfortunately, both can bedevil you with problems. Not surprisingly, most of these difficulties center around the crank operator itself or the linkage and track mechanisms.

Before attempting any of the repairs shown here, study the drawings below. They should give you a general knowledge of how your windows open and close as well as familiarize you with window terminology. (Note: With jalousie windows, except for routine repairs, call in a professional because much of the gear and lever mechanism is hidden from view.)

For help with repairing broken glass or screens, refer to pages 31-35. And if you need to plane off a high spot on a sash that is binding, see page 43 and follow the same general approach as that prescribed for binding doors.

Getting Balky Operator Mechanisms Operating Again

1 Start by opening the window far enough to disengage the arm from the track in which the arm slides. Clean both the track and the portion of the arm that connects to the

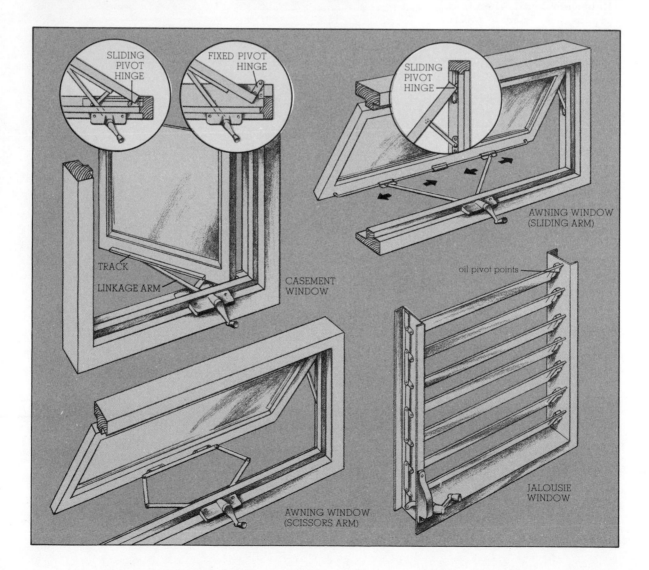

SLIDING PIVOT HINGE

FIXED PIVOT HINGE

SLIDING PIVOT HINGE

AWNING WINDOW (SLIDING ARM)

TRACK

LINKAGE ARM

CASEMENT WINDOW

oil pivot points

JALOUSIE WINDOW

AWNING WINDOW (SCISSORS ARM)

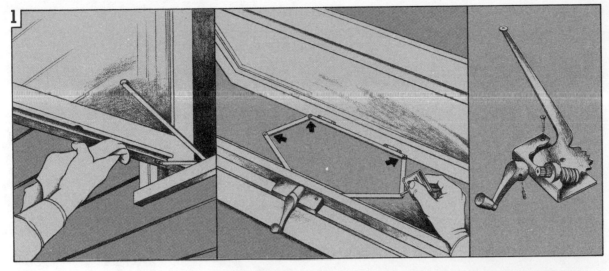

track with a rag or a cotton swab soaked in alcohol or in some cleaning liquid. Lubricate with a light grease or petroleum jelly.

Next, squeeze a penetrating oil into all pivot points and work the parts back and forth until things loosen up. Wipe up any excess oil.

The final step is to remove the operator itself, if possible, and coat the gears with a liberal amount of light grease. Replace the operator mechanism and see whether your effort has paid off.

Replacing an Operator

2 If no amount of cleaning or lubrication can make the window work smoothly, you may elect to replace the entire mechanism. To do this, open the window to the point where you can disengage the linkage arm from its track. Remove the screws holding the crank mechanism to the window frame, then slide out the entire assembly. Buy a replacement operator and install it, reversing the steps shown here.

Snugging Up a Sash

3 After lots of use, many crank-operated windows lose their ability to close tightly. Remedy this problem in either of the ways shown here. Installing weatherstripping is the easiest solution, but shimming works equally well.

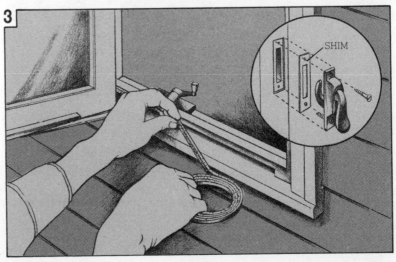

SHIM

DOORS

When a conscientious carpenter hangs doors during construction, he takes special care to ensure that they are plumb and square in their openings. Once the jambs are set and the doorknob and latch set have been installed, he verifies that the door opens and closes as it should and that the latch engages the strike plate correctly.

But that's at construction time. As time passes, the house settles, both the jamb and door itself expand and contract at different rates, and the door is opened and closed countless times. All of these factors (and others) eventually cause problems such

as binding doors and loose hinges. Although it is easy to put off door repairs until "next weekend," consider this: Like a lot of household repairs, door problems usually have a way of growing worse with neglect. Left to run their course, they can be vexing as well as serious compromises to the security and energy efficiency of your home.

In this chapter we show you how to solve several common hinged-door problems. Then we tell how to keep your sliding doors sliding, and conclude with help for balky garage doors—including tips for heading off problems before they start.

Repairing Hinged Doors

When a hinged door at your house starts to act up, don't immediately pull it off its hinges and whittle away its edges with a sanding block or a plane. Instead, with the door closed, inspect its perimeter and analyze what's causing the problem. Often you can make the repair with the door in place by adjusting the hinges, stops, or strike plate.

Freeing a Binding Door

1 If your door is binding near the top or bottom of the latch edge, first make sure that the hinge leaves on the door or jamb aren't loose (turn to page 44 for help with loose hinges). No problem there? Then you may be able to solve your problem by shimming out one of the hinges. Note: Shim the top hinge to cure a bind near the bottom, and shim the bottom hinge for binds near the top.

To shim out a hinge, open the door and insert a wedge beneath the latch edge for support. Then remove the screws that hold the hinge to the door jamb. Trim a piece of thin cardboard to fit the rectangular mortise on the door jamb, and insert the shim between the jamb and the hinge leaf.

2 If shimming takes care of the bind on the latch edge but causes the door to bind at the top or bottom, or if your only problem is binding at the top or bottom, pinpoint the location of the trouble spot while opening and closing the door. Scribe a line along the door's face to denote where you want to remove wood. If the bind is along the top edge, partially open the door, drive a wedge under its latch edge, and use a block plane to remove the high spot. Work from the end toward the center to avoid splintering the end grain.

3 If the high spot is on the door's bottom edge or along the hinge edge, take the door off its hinges for planing. With a hammer and a pry bar, tap up on the head of the hinge pins as shown.

Anchor the door in a floor-standing work vise. Hold it firm by wedging one end in a corner or by straddling it, and plane high spots. Then, for side planing, work a jack plane in the direction of the grain, holding it at a slight angle to the door. If you're planing end grain at the door's bottom edge, use a block plane and shave from the door's ends toward the center.

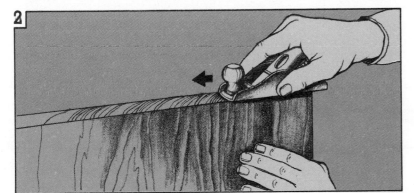

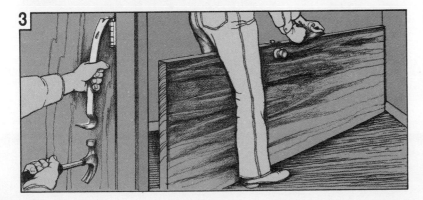

Dealing with Loose and Squeaky Hinges

1 Doors that sag or bind because of hinge-leaf screws that over time have worked loose in their holes and lost their grip are relatively easy to fix, and you needn't remove the door to do it. You should, however, open the door fully and tap a wedge of wood under the bottom of the latch edge with a hammer. This allows you to remove one hinge leaf without putting undue stress on the other hinge(s).

Now remove the loose hinge-leaf screws and determine whether the leaf will accept larger-diameter screws. If it will, install them and retighten the hinge.

If it won't, you can reuse the original screws if you provide a sound foundation in which to drive them. To do this, drill out the enlarged screw holes with a 1/4-inch bit and hammer in lengths of glue-coated 1/4-inch dowel. Then reposition the hinge leaf and secure it by driving the screws into the dowels.

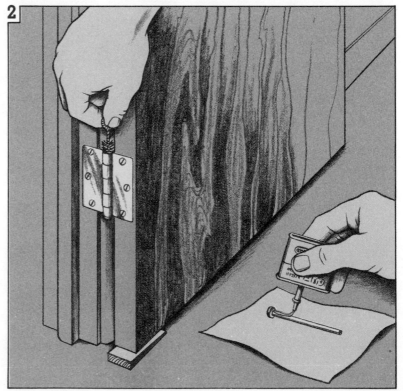

2 If your hinges are tight but noisy, here's how to eliminate annoying squeaks and reduce the unnecessary hinge wear that corrosion can cause. First, pry up the hinge pin 1/4 inch or so and squirt a few drops of light oil down into the barrel portion of the hinge. Have a rag handy to catch excess oil. Swing the door back and forth several times.

If the hinge continues to squeak, open the door fully, drive a wood wedge under the hinge side, and remove the pin. Clean any rust from the pin with steel wool, and from the barrel portion of the hinge using a stiff, pipecleaner-type wire brush. Apply a light coat of oil to the pin and replace it. (Don't drive the head of the pin all the way onto the hinge; leave a little space under it for easier removal next time.)

Curing Strike and Latch Problems

When your door closes but won't latch, it's a safe bet that your latch and strike plate aren't seeing eye to eye. Since it's impractical to tamper with the location of the latch in the door, you must make adjustments at the *strike plate* in the jamb.

1 If your latch and strike plate aren't engaging, examine the latch as the door closes to see which edge of the plate opening is causing it to hang up. (Scratches on the plate may already tell you.) If the two are off by no more than $\frac{1}{8}$ inch, remove the strike plate, anchor it in a vise, and file down the appropriate edge with a flat metal file. You also may need to chisel a larger opening in the door jamb to provide clearance for the latch.

2 If the latch and plate are off by more than $\frac{1}{8}$ inch, adjust the location of the plate in the jamb. Do this by extending the mortise in the proper direction.

To do this, score the edges of the extension to the proper depth with a sharp wood chisel and a hammer. Hold the chisel perpendicular to the jamb, with its bevel toward the mortise. Now reverse the direction of the bevel and work from inside the mortise to remove the rest of the wood, holding the chisel at about a 30-degree angle.

When a latch doesn't extend far enough into the strike plate, shim out the plate using the technique shown in sketch 1 on page 43.

3 Here's what to do when your door doesn't close far enough for the latch to engage. (This technique can also tighten the fit of a door that rattles in its frame.) Pry off the stop molding, allow the door to latch, and draw a line on the jamb to indicate where the stop molding needs to be. Reinstall the stop molding along this line. Finish the repair by painting or staining the bare wood you've uncovered.

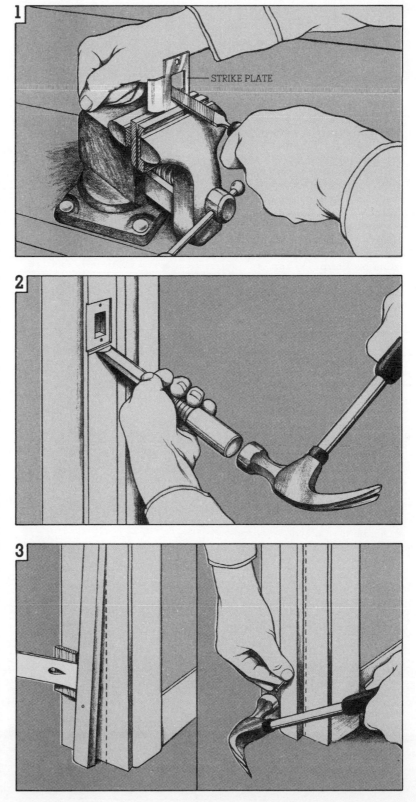

STRIKE PLATE

Repairing Sliding Doors

There are two popular kinds of sliding doors. *Patio doors,* the heavy, glass, exterior type, typically provide access to a deck or patio. They slide on rollers mounted on the bottom of the door frame. *By-pass doors,* the lightweight wooden interior doors, "hang" from rollers that slide in a top-mounted track.

Both types use self-lubricating nylon rollers that minimize problems. When something does go wrong, it's usually due to an obstruction in the track or a bend in a track or guide—each of which is easy to remedy.

Patio Doors

1 The bottom track along which patio doors glide is a natural trap for dirt, leaves, and other debris that interfere with door operation. Keep the track free of obstructions and the door smooth-running by periodically loosening any accumulated dirt with a whisk broom. Then use the hose attachment of a vacuum for final cleanup.

2 Although the nylon rollers on sliding patio doors are self-lubricating, you can further ease their travel by puffing powdered graphite along the track. Rubbing track surfaces with paraffin also works.

3 When a patio door "hangs up," also inspect the track for a bent channel. Often, you can restore smooth operation by tapping out the bend with a hammer and a wooden block.

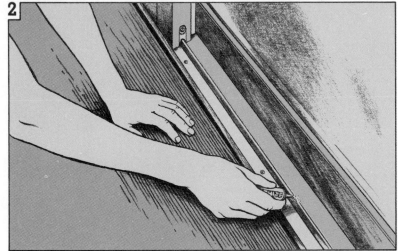

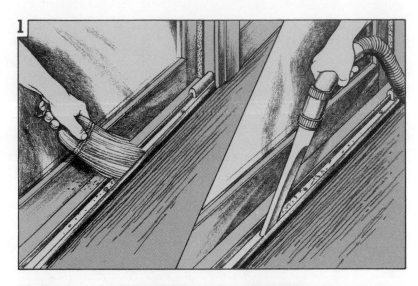

4 If a door hangs up because it is not sliding squarely on its rollers, adjust the rollers up or down to bring the door into alignment. Find the access plug at the bottom of the panel and turn its screw clockwise to raise the rollers, counterclockwise to lower them.

5 Sometimes your door will glide smoothly but its latch will fail to engage at the catch in the jamb. When that happens, loosen the catch screws and move the catch up or down in its slide-mount until it is properly aligned with the latch. (With some brands of doors, there is an adjustment screw on the door that you turn to adjust the latch.)

Bypass Doors

Fortunately, you can correct most jamming, track-jumping, or misalignment problems with bypass doors by adjusting the rollers or the door guides. Remove the door from its track and make the checks described below.

1 To remove a bypass door, first remove the screws that hold the door's floor guide in place. Then, swing the bottom of the door hung on the front track toward you. Note: With some models you need to position the rollers at a "keyed opening" before removing the door.

2 Inspect the roller brackets to see whether they have loosened and come out of original alignment. Reposition them in their slotted slide mounts and tighten their screws. (In extreme cases where the screw holes are stripped, move the brackets to the left or right slightly.) Correctly placed brackets will allow the door to clear the floor by at least ⅜ inch.

3 Check the floor guides and replace any that are broken or hopelessly bent. If a metal guide is only slightly bent, you may be able to restore it to operation by straightening it with a pair of pliers or a wooden block and hammer.

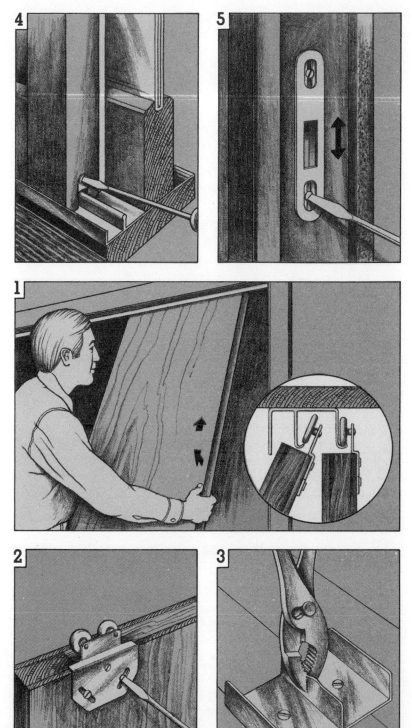

Repairing Garage Doors

A smoothly operating garage door is something we too often take for granted. At no time is this more evident than the morning it suddenly refuses to open.

When garage door problems do occur, they usually result from damage caused by moisture or lack of proper maintenance. Moisture—some of it unavoidable—may have warped the door, rusted its hardware, or even rotted away an entire section of framing members that hold it in alignment. Or maybe you've allowed the door's brackets to loosen or its tracks to become clogged with dirt and grime.

A periodic maintenance routine is your best insurance against garage door difficulties. This consists of nothing more than keeping the track clean, keeping the hardware lubricated, and tightening any nuts or hold-down bolts that may have worked loose. You might be surprised at how these measures head off most overhead door problems.

1 When your garage door binds as it travels on its track, it may be because the track brackets have loosened and the tracks are no longer parallel to each other. You can easily check this by measuring the distance between them with a tape measure at several points. If the tracks are out of alignment, loosen the appropriate track brackets, tap the tracks back into parallel alignment with a couple of good hammer blows (making sure that the vertical tracks are plumb), and retighten the brackets.

2 If your door binds just as it starts to open or tries to close completely and its tracks are tight and parallel, check to see whether the edges are rubbing on the inside surface of the trim molding. Sometimes abrasions at the edges of the door's face will indicate this. One way to correct this problem is to remove the outside trim molding and reinstall it slightly farther from the door to provide more clearance.

Another (often easier) way is to relocate the vertical tracks farther from the trim molding. If the bracket isn't adjustable, remove the lag screws holding the track brackets in place and reinstall the brackets with wood-block shims inserted between the brackets and the framing members. If yours are adjustable, simply loosen the bolts and make the needed adjustment.

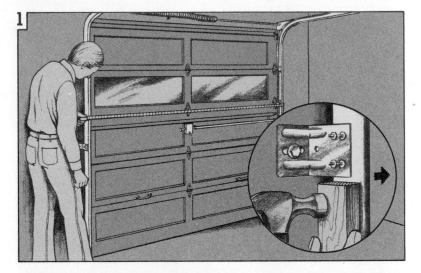

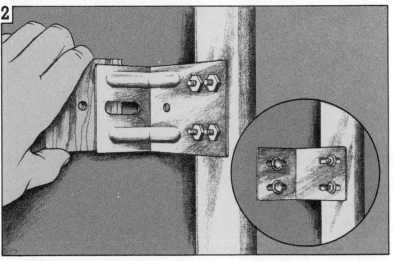

3 Perhaps the simplest garage door adjustment you can make is correcting a bar lock that fails to key into the track. You can easily move the bar lock guides up or down in their slide mounts to bring the bar into alignment.

4 Even a garage door that operates smoothly may need rebalancing from time to time. Indications of this are when the door opens or closes too easily or won't stay in its opened position. A properly balanced garage door should stay open when it's about three feet off the driveway. Above that point it should slowly rise to its fully opened position; below that point it should slowly close.

If your garage door fails to open in the way mentioned here, the springs that pull the door open probably have lost tension and need tightening. These springs are fully stretched when the door is closed, and under the least tension when it's fully open. So when you make the following adjustments, open the door fully to relax the springs, and secure there.

With some *spring tension* mechanisms, one end of the spring attaches to one of the holes in a bracket attached to the door jamb. You can increase spring tension by hooking the spring into a higher hole (you may need to remove the cable from the other end of the spring to do this). Adjust the spring on each side of the door equally to keep balanced tension.

With other spring tension mechanisms, you can add stretch to the spring by taking up slack in the cable that holds the spring's pulley connector. Take up cable slack (on both sides) about an inch at a time until you achieve the right balance.

Yet a third mechanism is known as a *torsion spring.* Unless you've had prior experience adjusting this type of door, call in a qualified serviceman to balance it for you. The torsion spring is under tremendous pressure, and is potentially dangerous if improperly handled.

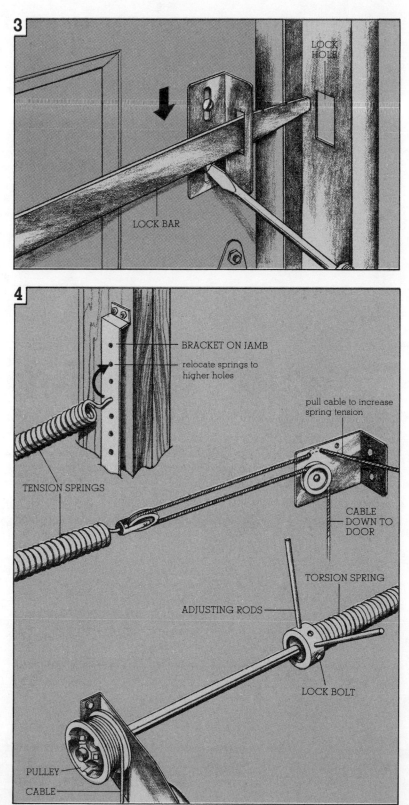

3

LOCK HOLE

LOCK BAR

4

BRACKET ON JAMB

relocate springs to higher holes

pull cable to increase spring tension

TENSION SPRINGS

CABLE DOWN TO DOOR

TORSION SPRING

ADJUSTING RODS

LOCK BOLT

PULLEY

CABLE

ELECTRICAL REPAIRS

Many do-it-yourselfers, even those who are undaunted by almost any other type of repair, step out of the picture when it comes to dealing with things electrical. For even the most minor repair they prefer to call in an electrician and confine their involvement to household fixups that "don't bite back."

Make no mistake about it. Electricity is potentially dangerous, and it does demand your respect. But you can say the same thing about your electric drill and even your hammer. So, to minimize the potential risks involved, heed the following safety rule: *Before you work on any circuit, shut off the power and use a testing device to make sure it's off.*

In this chapter we guide you step by step through the most common household electrical problems you're likely to encounter, from troubleshooting tripped circuit breakers and blown fuses to dealing with problem plugs and cords, switches and receptacles, light fixtures, and even door chimes.

Troubleshooting Tripped Circuit Breakers

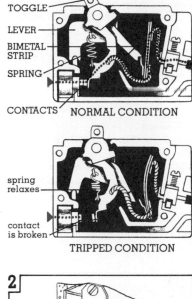

TOGGLE
LEVER
BIMETAL STRIP
SPRING
CONTACTS   NORMAL CONDITION

spring relaxes
contact is broken

TRIPPED CONDITION

Think of a circuit breaker as a heat-sensing, spring-loaded switch. The cutaway drawings at right show one of these sensitive devices in its normal and tripped states.

When the *toggle* is "on," current flows through a set of *contacts* held together by a *spring* and *lever.* These are kept in tension by a *bimetal strip,* which is part of the circuit's current flow.

If something goes awry in the circuit—either a short or an overload—the bimetal heats up, bends, and the spring separates the contacts.

Once current stops, the bimetal cools and tries to straighten again, but it's not strong enough to stretch the spring, so the contacts remain open until the toggle is manually reset.

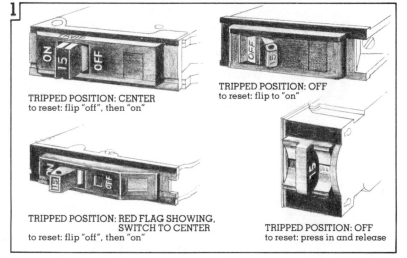

TRIPPED POSITION: CENTER
to reset: flip "off", then "on"

TRIPPED POSITION: OFF
to reset: flip to "on"

TRIPPED POSITION: RED FLAG SHOWING, SWITCH TO CENTER
to reset: flip "off", then "on"

TRIPPED POSITION: OFF
to reset: press in and release

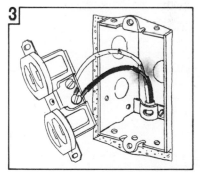

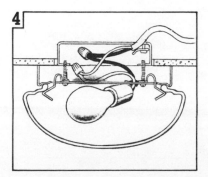

A tripped breaker may identify itself in any of the four ways shown above. To find out whether the problem that caused the outage has corrected itself, reset the breaker. Don't worry about shock or fire. If there's still a short or overload, the breaker will snap off again.

Overloads are easy to correct. Usually you only need to unplug or turn off one of the circuit's bigger electricity users.

If that doesn't help, suspect a short. To locate one, systematically unplug items until the breaker holds. A defective plug, cord, or lamp socket may be the culprit (see pages 54-57).

2 Short circuits can occur in outlet boxes, too. Here, a wire has pulled loose from the switch and shorted out against the box.

3 Frayed or cracked insulation can expose a wire and cause a short. The solution: Wrap it with several layers of electrical tape.

4 High-wattage bulbs in a light fixture can melt insulation and produce a short. Never use bulbs larger than those for which the fixture is rated. More about troubleshooting light fixtures on pages 60-63.

Troubleshooting Blown Fuses

If yours is an older home that hasn't been rewired, chances are its electrical "heart" is a fuse box rather than a breaker box. Fuses and circuit breakers serve exactly the same purpose, but instead of tripping as a breaker does, a fuse "blows" when too much current is in its circuit. Then you must eliminate the short or overload (see page 51), remove the blown fuse, and replace it.

Refer to the anatomy drawing below and note that once again power comes in via a couple of *main power cables.* (In a house with no 240-volt equipment, there may be only one of these.)

Next, current flows through a main disconnect, in this case a *pullout block* that holds a pair of *cartridge fuses.*

Next in line are a series of *plug fuses* that protect the black "hot" wires of branch circuits. Unscrewing one of these disconnects its circuit.

1 Peer closely through the window of a plug fuse and you'll see a strip of metal through which current flows. The intense heat of a short or an overload causes this strip to melt, disconnecting the circuit.

Often just looking at a plug fuse can tell you whether a short or an overload caused it to blow. A short circuit explodes the strip, blackening the fuse window. An overload, on the other hand, usually leaves the window clear.

2 Cartridge fuses, such as those you might find on the back of a main or 240-volt pullout, can't be checked visually. To determine whether one has blown, either install a new one or check the old one with a continuity tester as shown. The bulb will light if the fuse is good.

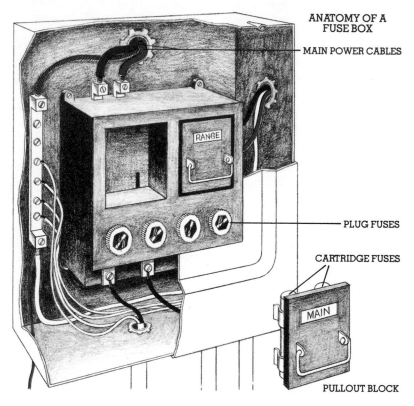

ANATOMY OF A FUSE BOX

MAIN POWER CABLES

PLUG FUSES

CARTRIDGE FUSES

PULLOUT BLOCK

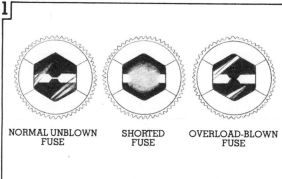

NORMAL UNBLOWN FUSE

SHORTED FUSE

OVERLOAD-BLOWN FUSE

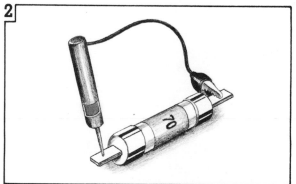

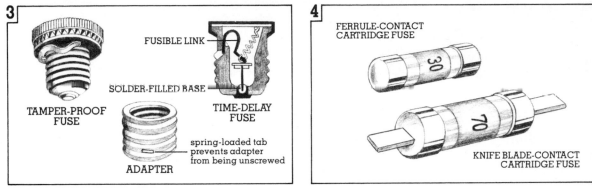

3 TAMPER-PROOF FUSE — FUSIBLE LINK — SOLDER-FILLED BASE — TIME-DELAY FUSE — ADAPTER — spring-loaded tab prevents adapter from being unscrewed

4 FERRULE-CONTACT CARTRIDGE FUSE — KNIFE BLADE-CONTACT CARTRIDGE FUSE

3 Ordinary plug fuses are interchangeable regardless of their amperage ratings. **So if you have a chronically overloaded circuit, you might be tempted to install a "bigger" fuse. Don't do it. Wiring that gets more current than it was designed to handle heats up and can catch fire.**

Tamper-proof fuses make it impossible for you or anyone else to "overfuse" a circuit. Each comes with a threaded *adapter* that fits permanently into the box. The adapter accepts only a fuse of the proper rating.

Another problem with ordinary plug fuses is that they can be blown by even the momentary overload that often happens when an electric motor starts up. A *time-delay* fuse waits a second or so. If the overload continues, its *solder-filled* base melts and shuts down the circuit. A short then blows the *fusible link*, just as it would in any other fuse.

4 Circuits rated at 30 to 60 amps typically use *ferrule-contact* cartridge fuses. *Knife blade-contact* fuses handle 70 amps or more. Both must be handled with extreme caution. Touching either end of a live one could give you a potentially fatal shock.

5 For safety, keep a plastic *fuse puller* with your spare fuses, and use it as shown at right. Note, too, that the ends of a cartridge fuse get hot, so don't touch them even after you've pulled the fuse.

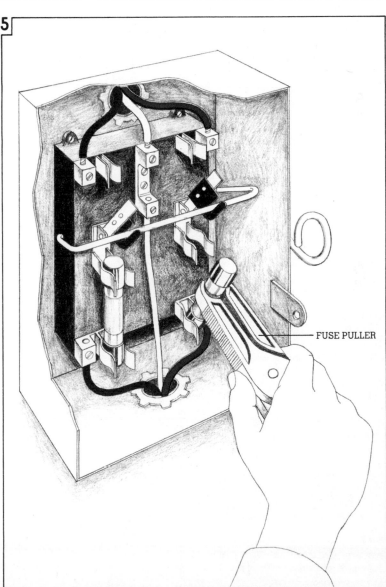

5 FUSE PULLER

Replacing Plugs, Cords, and Lamp Sockets

Have you ever been jolted by an electrical shock? If so, it probably came from a faulty plug, cord, or lamp socket. They pose the most common shock and fire hazards.

Fortunately, they're also far and away the easiest to repair. Master just a few basics and you can make short work of any potential short circuit.

Plugs get stepped on, bumped against, and yanked out by their cords. Even properly handled ones eventually wear out. So glance at any plug before you use it. If it shows signs of damage, replace it immediately.

The drawing at right shows some of the plug variations you'll find. *Round-cord* and *flat-cord* plugs are suitable for lamps, radios, and other low-amperage users. Newer lamp and extension cord plugs are *polarized*; one blade is wider than the other.

Heaters, irons, and similar appliances pull more current and require heftier plugs; 240-volt equipment calls for special blade configurations.

Cords vary, too. *Zip cord*, the most common, should be used only for light duty. Twisted cords have two layers of insulation. *Heater cords* are triple-insulated, as is the heavy-duty, three-wire type required to ground appliances and other equipment. The *240-volt cords* have three fatter wires.

Lamp sockets come with a variety of different switching mechanisms. Most have brass-plated shells.

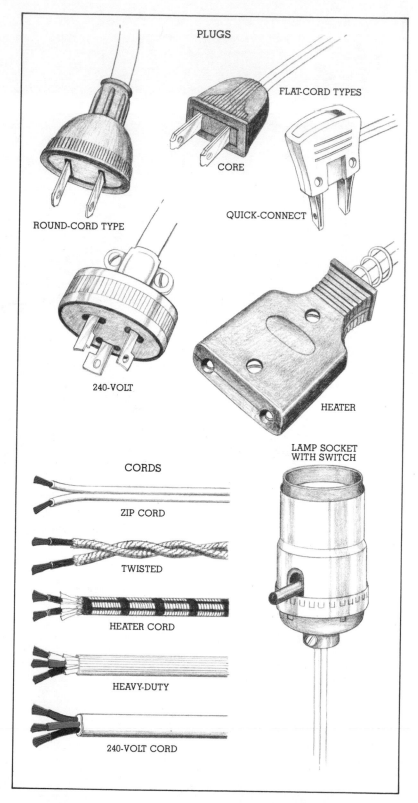

PLUGS

FLAT-CORD TYPES

CORE

QUICK-CONNECT

ROUND-CORD TYPE

240-VOLT

HEATER

LAMP SOCKET WITH SWITCH

CORDS

ZIP CORD

TWISTED

HEATER CORD

HEAVY-DUTY

240-VOLT CORD

Replacing Plugs

Round-Cord Plugs

1 Begin by snipping off the old plug, slipping a new one onto the cord, and stripping away insulation as shown.

2 Now tie the "Underwriters' knot" so that tugging the cord can't loosen the electrical connections you'll be making. Always try to protect connections from stress.

3 Twist the wire strands tight with your fingers. Then, with a pair of long-nose pliers, shape clockwise hooks like these.

4 As you tighten the screws, tuck in any stray strands. If the screws differ, attach the black or ribbed wire to the brass one.

5 Finally, check to be sure all wires and strands are neatly inside the plug's shell, then slip on the cardboard cover.

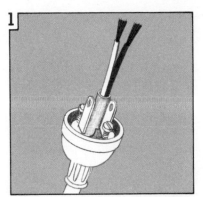

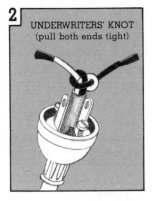

UNDERWRITERS' KNOT
(pull both ends tight)

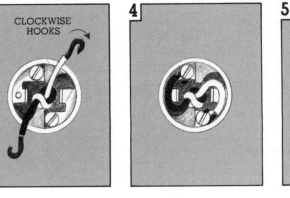

CLOCKWISE HOOKS

Flat-Cord Plugs

Flat-cord plugs connect in a variety of ways. Some require the same procedure shown above. Others have a core that you attach the wires to, then snap into a shell, as depicted here. Still another core type bites into unstripped cord, as the quick-connect plug shown on page 56 does.

1 First slip the shell onto the cord, peel apart the wires, and strip away about half an inch of plastic insulation.

2 Twist the strands and form clockwise hooks big enough to wrap three-fourths of the way around each screw.

3 Slip the wires under the plug's screws, then tighten the screws to secure the connection.

4 Now just snap the core into the shell. With practice, the entire job takes only minutes. *(continued)*

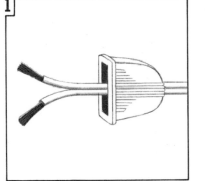

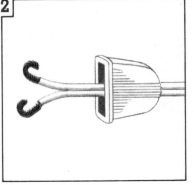

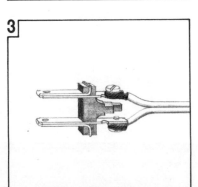

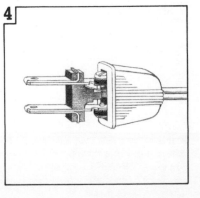

Replacing Plugs *(contd.)*

Quick-Connect Plugs

Keep a few quick-connect plugs on hand and you'll never again be tempted to put off replacing a faulty or questionable plug. Installing one takes about as long as changing a light bulb, and the only tool you need is a sharp knife or pair of scissors.

1 Snip off the old plug. Lift the lever on top of the new plug and insert the zip cord at the side.

2 Closing the lever pierces and holds the wire. It's that easy.

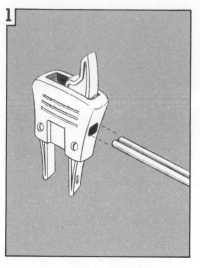
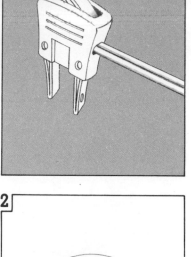

240-Volt Plug

Really just an oversized round-cord plug with an extra blade, a 240-volt plug installs in much the same way. You don't have to tie an Underwriters' knot, however. A steel clamp grips the cord.

1 Slide the plug onto the cord and strip the three wires as shown. Twist the strands tightly together and form hooks.

2 Attach the black and red wires to brass-colored terminals, and the green wire to the silver-colored screw. Tuck everything into place, tighten the cord clamp, and slip on the cardboard cover.

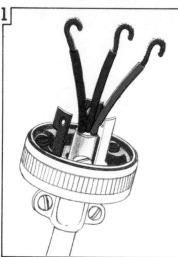
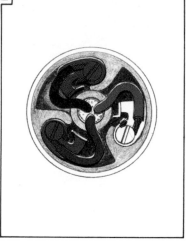

Heater Plugs

Wall plugs for heaters, irons, and other "hot" appliances typically are molded to the cord. To replace the plug, it's best to replace the cord as well. You may be able to replace the female plug at the cord's other end, depending on whether it comes apart.

1 If your plug is like the one shown, it will pull apart once you loosen the screws. Note how the spring relieves strain on the cord.

2 If the plug has a brass terminal, connect the black wire to it and the white wire to the silver one. Clips tie the plug to the heater blades.

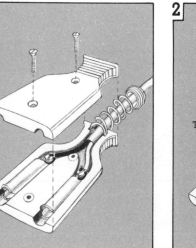
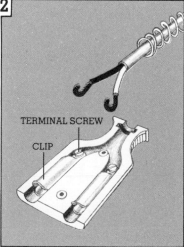

Replacing Cords

Lamp and appliance cord must be sized according to the load it will carry. For lamps, clocks, and other items that draw less than 7 amps, use No. 18 wire; 7- to 10-amp appliances need No. 16 wire; anything larger than 10 amps should have a No. 14 cord. The larger the wire number, the smaller its size.

1 You'll probably have to dismantle part of the unit to find out how its cord hooks in. Expect to find screw terminals, solder connections, or solderless connectors that screw on or crimp on.

2 Release a soldered connection as shown here. To resolder, insert the wire, heat the entire connection, including the terminal, then touch solder to it. The solder will melt and fuse the joint.

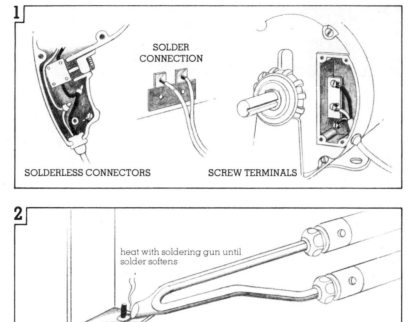

Replacing Lamp Sockets

When a lamp won't work and you know its bulb is OK, unplug the cord and pry up the little brass contact in the socket base. If this doesn't bring results, or if the cardboard insulation has deteriorated, replace the socket.

While you're at it, you might want to install a new cord and plug (a polarized one). The easiest way to thread new cord through a lamp base is to tie it to the old one with a piece of string. As you withdraw the old, the new will follow it.

1 Examine the socket shell and you'll find the word *press*. Push hard here and the unit will pull apart into the series of components illustrated.

2 Slip the new socket base onto the cord, tie it with an Underwriters' knot, and attach wires to each of the terminals. Reassemble everything and the job is done.

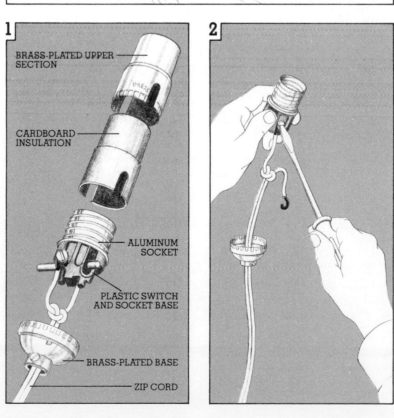

Replacing Switches and Receptacles

Tired of pampering a balky switch or a paint-glopped receptacle that holds plugs with only the feeblest of grips? Armed with just a screwdriver, a neon test light, and the know-how explained on these two pages, you can install a new one in 15 minutes or less, and that includes time for a couple of trips to your service panel to cut and restore power. That's because all you have to do is wire the new device the way the old one was wired.

To be safe, always de-energize a switch or receptacle before you touch its inner workings. To do this, you'll need to shut off your home's main circuit breaker or pull its main disconnect fuse block. Or deactivate only the circuit you think you'll be working on, then check the condition of the circuit with a test light, as shown here. Note, however, that to test a switch, you must have a·good bulb in the fixture it controls.

Switches

1 Is the circuit live? With the switch off, touch the tester's probes to its screw terminals. If the light glows, the circuit is still hot.

2 If the tester doesn't light, remove the screws holding the switch's ears to the box and pull out the device. Now loosen the screw terminals and disconnect the wires.

3 A three-way switch has three terminals. Note which is marked or otherwise identified as the *common* before you unhook the wire. This terminal may not be in the same place on your new switch.

4 Some new switches have push-in terminals in back as well as screws on the sides. If you use screws, wrap wires around them in a clockwise direction.

5 Now tuck the wires and switch back into the box and tighten the hold-down screws. Don't force anything; switches crack easily.

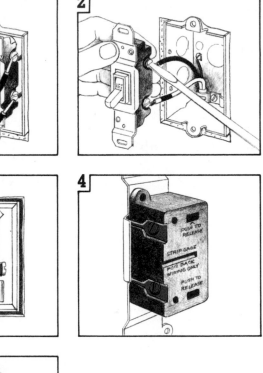

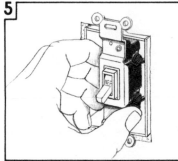

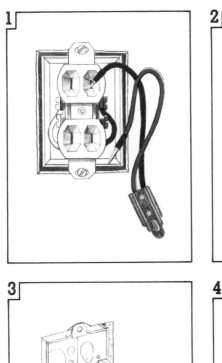

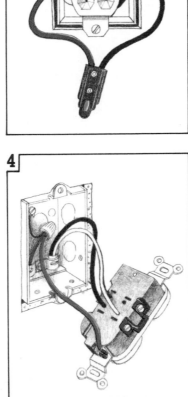

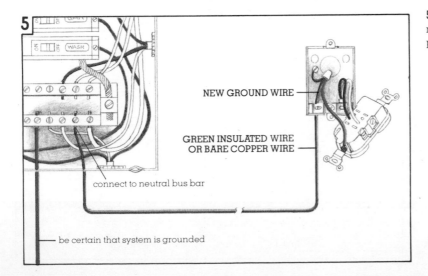

NEW GROUND WIRE

GREEN INSULATED WIRE
OR BARE COPPER WIRE

connect to neutral bus bar

be certain that system is grounded

Receptacles

1 Can you replace a two-slot, non-grounding receptacle with a safer, three-hole version? To find out, remove the wall plate, leave power on, and touch one probe of the tester to the receptacle strap or the box. Now insert the other probe into each of the slots. If either lights up the tester, the box itself is grounded and you can install a three-hole type. If not, either get a two-slot receptacle or — better yet — run a separate ground as shown in the bottom sketch on this page.

2 To learn whether a receptacle is live, touch the tester probes to screws on either side. The light will glow if there's power.

3 Remove the hold-down screws and pull out the device. Be sure to note which wires are attached to which terminals before unfastening them.

4 Newer receptacles have push-in terminals as well as screws. Whichever you use, connect white wires to silver, black to brass. If you find a bare wire inside the box, ground the receptacle's green screw to it and to the box with a couple of short green wires. If there is no bare wire but you know the box is grounded, run a jumper directly from the receptacle to the box.

5 To ground an ungrounded box, run a wire from it to the service panel or to a cold water pipe.

Troubleshooting Incandescent Fixtures

Incandescent fixtures vary widely in style, but most have some arrangement of the components illustrated in the anatomy drawing at right.

A *canopy plate* attaches to a wall or ceiling fixture box, and also supports a *bulb holder* that consists of one or more *sockets. Leads* connect the sockets to wiring in the box.

To get at the bulbs, you usually must remove some sort of translucent glass or plastic *diffuser.* Most manufacturers post a maximum wattage on the canopy. Bulbs of a wattage higher than the recommended rating generate too much heat, which is the main enemy of incandescent fixtures.

When a fixture shorts out, you can almost be certain that the problem lies in the fixture itself or in its electrical box. If a fixture refuses to light, however, the switch that controls it could be faulty.

(Note: Be sure to shut off power before beginning.)

1 Carefully inspect the socket. If you find cracks, scorching, or melting, it should be replaced. You can find a new one at a lamp store.

If the socket is intact and securely mounted to the canopy plate, remove the bulb and check the contact at the socket's base. If there's corrosion, turn off the circuit — not just the switch — and scrape the contact with a screwdriver or steel wool. Also pry up the contact a bit.

2 If the problem remains, shut off the circuit again and drop the fixture from its outlet box. To do this, remove either a single nut in the center or a pair of screws located off-center. Now check for loose connections and for cut, frayed, or melted insulation. Wrap any bare wires with electrical tape.

ANATOMY OF AN INCANDESCENT CEILING FIXTURE

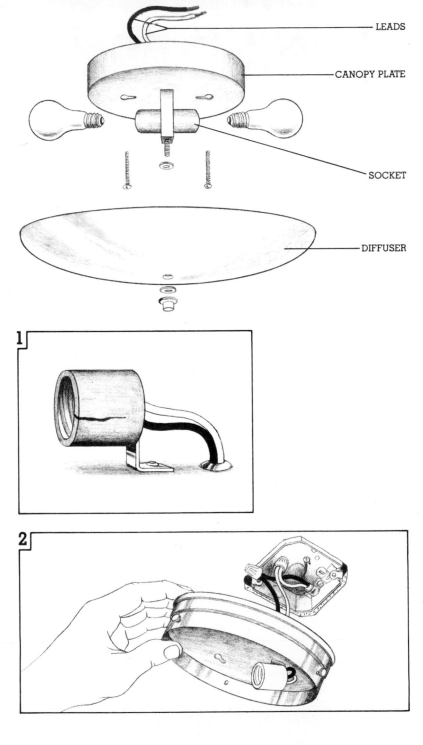

LEADS

CANOPY PLATE

SOCKET

DIFFUSER

Testing Switches

1 Internal switches on a fixture or lamp usually are connected with a pair of small pressure connectors. **To test the switch, unplug the lamp and remove the connectors holding the switch's leads.** Leave the bare wires twisted together but arrange them so the connections aren't touching each other or anything else.

Restore power to the lamp or fixture and carefully touch your tester to the connections. Now flip the switch and test again. If the tester lights, the switch is bad.

2 To test a wall switch, turn it to the "on" position and touch the tester to the terminal screws. Here, too, if the tester lights, the switch must be replaced, as shown on page 58.

3 Nervous about poking into a live switch? Then shut down its circuit and conduct your investigation with a continuity tester. In the above situations, the tester should light when the switch is on, but not when it is off. If you get a glow in both positions or no glow in either position, you need a new switch.

To check out a three-way switch such as this one, shut off the circuit and attach the tester's clip to the common terminal; it is usually identified on the switch body. Now touch the probe to one of the other terminals and flip the switch. If it's OK, the tester will light in one position or the other. Repeat this test with the other terminal.

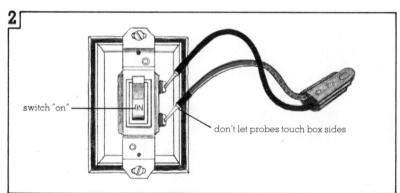

if tester lights, replace the switch

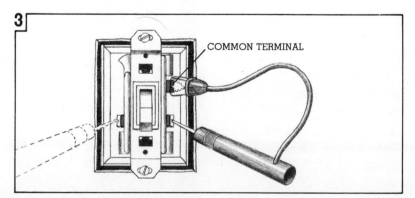

switch "on"

don't let probes touch box sides

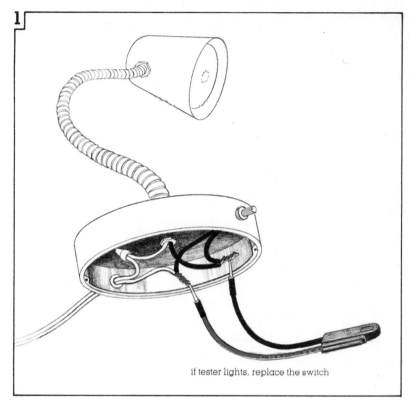

COMMON TERMINAL

Troubleshooting Fluorescent Fixtures

Switching on an ordinary light bulb charges a metal filament that literally burns with white heat. Fluorescent tubes, on the other hand, don't get nearly as hot because they operate in a different way.

Anatomically (see sketch below), the heart of a fluorescent fixture is its *ballast,* an electrical transformer that steps up voltage and then sends it to a pair of *lamp holders.* The current from the lamp holders excites a gas inside the tube, causing its phosphorus-coated inner surface to glow with cool, diffused light.

Because they produce far less heat, fluorescent tubes last much longer than incandescent bulbs and consume considerably less electrical energy. Problems are fewer, too. Following are the major ills you're likely to encounter with fluorescent fixtures.

ANATOMY OF A RAPID-START FLUORESCENT LIGHT

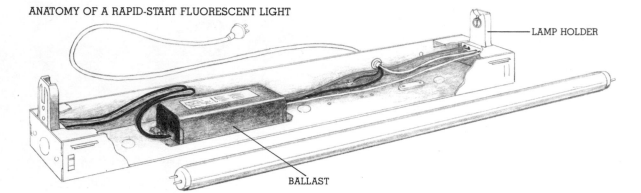

LAMP HOLDER

BALLAST

1 Rarely do fluorescent tubes burn out abruptly. When a tube won't light, try wiggling its ends to be sure they're properly seated.

If this doesn't get things glowing again and yours is a rapid-start tube like the one shown, suspect a loose or broken connection. **Start your search by turning off power to the circuit,** removing the tubes and the fixture cover, and inspecting all connections inside. Next, check the switch (see page 61 for details).

2 As a last resort, you may have to drop the entire fixture and look for loose connections and broken or bare wires in the outlet box.

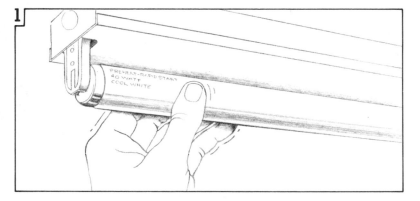

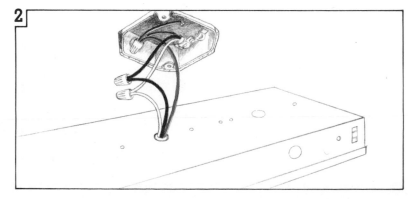

3 When a tube begins to fail, the normally grayish bands near its ends gradually blacken. Uniform dimming usually means the tube simply needs washing. When you shop for a new tube, select one of the same wattage as the old one.

4 Older, delayed-start fluorescent lights flicker momentarily as they light up. If the flickering continues, make sure the starter is seated by pushing it in and turning clockwise.

   When the ends of a tube light up but its center does not, the starter probably has gone bad. To remove it, press in and turn counterclockwise.

5 Humming, an acrid odor, or tarlike goop dripping from a fixture indicates that the ballast is going bad. To replace it, follow the procedures shown below. But first compare the price of a new ballast with that of a new fixture. It may be more economical to replace the entire unit.

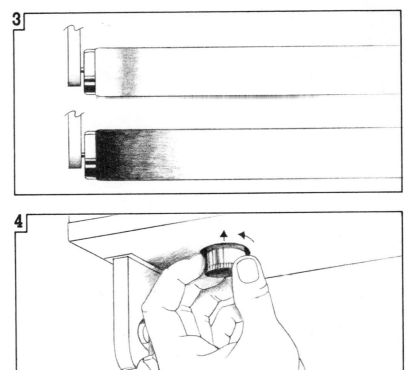

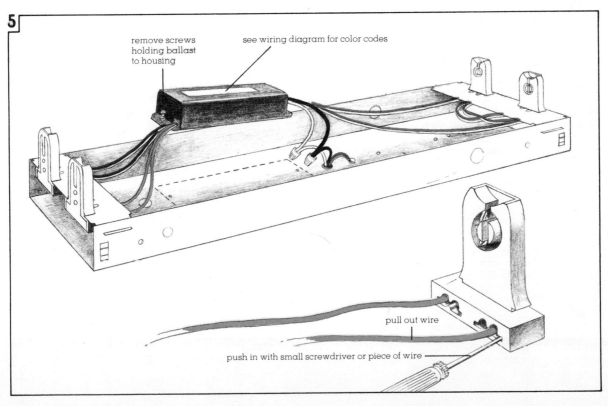

remove screws holding ballast to housing

see wiring diagram for color codes

pull out wire

push in with small screwdriver or piece of wire

Repairing a Silent Door Chime

Apprehensive about electricity's potential for fire and shock? You can put aside those fears when you work with door chimes, intercoms, thermostats, and even some lighting systems. Current for them flows in the same sort of circuits that serve the rest of your house, but at voltages that scarcely tickle.

Examine the chime systems shown at right and you'll see that everything starts with a *transformer,* which "steps down" 120-volt house current to one of several levels between six and 30 volts. From the transformer, light-gauge wire makes a circuit that is normally open. Pressing the button, which is a spring-loaded switch, closes the circuit, sending the lowered voltage to sound the chimes.

Troubleshooting low-voltage circuitry is a simple process of elimination. A voltmeter makes the job easier, but you can also do most tests with only a short length of wire or a screwdriver.

1 Weather and insistent delivery-men make buttons the most vulnerable parts of a chime system, so start your investigation there. To test a button, unscrew it and jump its terminals as shown. (You may have to scrape away corrosion first.) If the chimes sound, the button is faulty and should be replaced.

If the chimes don't sound, the problem is elsewhere. Disconnecting the button and twisting its wires together let you make the other tests shown on the opposite page without running back and forth to push the button.

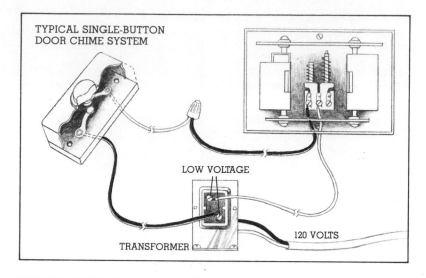

TYPICAL SINGLE-BUTTON DOOR CHIME SYSTEM

LOW VOLTAGE

TRANSFORMER

120 VOLTS

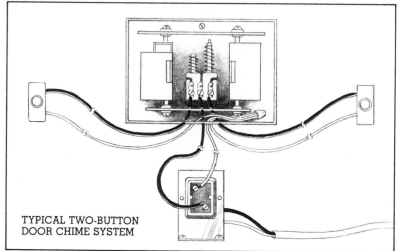

TYPICAL TWO-BUTTON DOOR CHIME SYSTEM

1

JUMP A WIRE ACROSS TERMINALS
(or use a screwdriver)

2 Next, take a look at the transformer. It may be situated at or near your home's service panel, or attached to a junction box in the vicinity of a door or the chimes themselves.

Here, one of the wires has come loose. Reconnecting it should ring the chimes.

3 Is the transformer working? To find out, disconnect both wires and check out each terminal with the probes of a voltmeter. If the meter shows no reading at all, the transformer is the culprit and must be replaced.

You also can test a transformer by jumping its low-voltage terminals with a screwdriver. If you see even a weak spark, the unit is OK. **Before disconnecting a dead transformer, be sure to shut off the household circuit it taps into. Here you're dealing with 120 volts, and all the usual cautions apply.**

4 If the transformer passes your tests, examine the chime unit itself. First look for any loose or broken connections.

Now, to check the front chimes of a two-button system, touch the voltmeter probes across the *front* and *trans* terminals. If the meter registers a reading, the chimes are shot. To test the rear chimes, touch the *rear* and *trans* terminals.

If you don't have a voltmeter, test the chimes by connecting them directly to the transformer. Good ones will ring.

If the button, transformer, and chimes all check out, a wire probably has broken somewhere. To find out for sure, disconnect the leads of the chime and test for current flow with the voltmeter, or jump the leads with a screwdriver and watch for a spark.

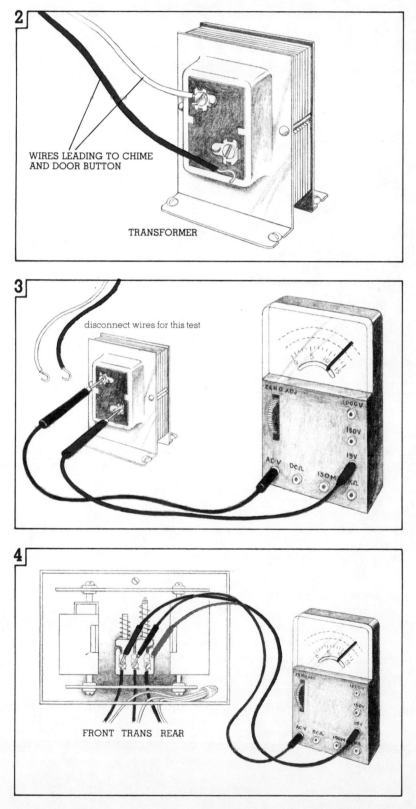

WIRES LEADING TO CHIME AND DOOR BUTTON

TRANSFORMER

disconnect wires for this test

FRONT TRANS REAR

PLUMBING REPAIRS

Does this sound familiar? Your stopped-up kitchen sink refuses to yield to repeated attacks with a plunger. Even that expensive drain cleaner you brought home from the store won't break through the blockage. You resign yourself to calling in a plumber, who spends 10 minutes working on your sink with a snake-like tool called a drain auger and puts you back in business.

This is the point at which it usually dawns on people that with the right tool they could have done the same thing for a fraction of the cost and had a drain auger of their own on hand to deal with the next such plumbing incident.

It's our hope that this section will save you from a frustration like the one recounted above. As you'll see, the key to success with most household plumbing repairs is knowing what needs to be done and knowing what specialized tools can help you do it. We show you both as they apply to most of the plumbing problems you'll encounter. Heading the list are clogged drains and traps, followed closely by leaky faucets. Rounding out this section are pages that deal with toilet repairs, food waste disposer problems, and leaky, noisy, or frozen pipes.

Opening Clogged Drains

If a fixture stops up, you'll naturally want to take immediate action. But before you rush at the problem with a plunger or an auger, take a moment to analyze where the blockage might be.

Typically, homes have three types of drains. *Fixture drains* have a trap and short sections of pipe on either side; *main drains* collect waste from all the fixture drains; and a *sewer drain* carries liquid and solid waste out of the house to a community sewer, cesspool, or septic tank.

Nine times out of ten, the problem will be close to a fixture. To verify your suspicions, check other drains in your home. If more than one won't clear, something is stuck in a main drain. If no drains work, the problem is farther down the line, and you'll have to continue your investigation.

Sinks and Lavatories

1 Clearing a sink or lavatory may involve nothing more than removing the strainer or stopper from the bowl's drain opening—a job that's generally as fast as it is easy. Bits of soap, hair, food matter, or other debris can be the culprit.

Kitchen sink strainer baskets simply lift out. Some lavatory stoppers do, too. (See page 73 for a look at a typical lavatory.) Others require a slight turn before lifting. With a few, you must reach under the sink and remove a pivot rod.

2 A plunger uses water pressure to blast out obstructions. This means its rubber cup must seal tightly around the drain opening before you begin working the handle up and down. (Water in the bowl helps create this seal.) Stuff a rag in the overflow outlet of lavatories so the pressure can build and free the blocked passage.

3 If plunging doesn't work, fit an auger down the drain. Cranking its handle rotates a stiff spring that bores through a stubborn blockage. If this doesn't get results, dismantle the trap as shown on page 72 and auger the drainpipe that goes into the wall or floor.

Note: Chemical cleaners can sometimes speed up a slow-draining sink or lavatory, but avoid dumping them into one that is totally clogged. If they don't clear the drain, your problem is compounded by dangerously caustic water.

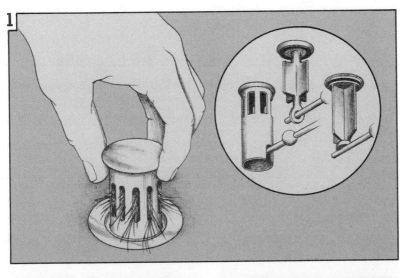

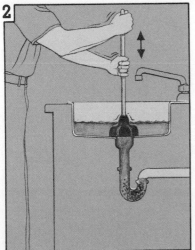

Opening Clogged Drains *(continued)*

Tubs and Showers

1 If a tub drain clogs, reach first for your plunger. If your tub has a *pop-up stopper,* you must remove it before plunging. Wiggling helps free the floppy linkage assembly.

Before you plunge, plug up the overflow and allow an inch or so of water to accumulate in the tub. This helps seal the rubber cup around the tub outlet. As you work the plunger up and down, you will hear water surging back and forth in the drain.

2 If plunging doesn't do the trick, thread in an auger. If there's no stopper in evidence, you have a *trip-lever assembly* like the one illustrated below, left. With this type, pry up or unscrew the *strainer* so you can insert the auger.

If you can get only a few inches of the auger into the drain and that doesn't clear it, then the problem is in the tub's trap directly below the overflow. To clear it, you'll have to follow a different route.

The best way to approach most tub traps is down through the *overflow tube.* This involves removing the pop-up or trip-lever assembly, which you do by unscrewing the overflow plate and pulling out the conglomeration of parts attached to it. (For more information about pop-up and trip-lever assemblies, turn to page 73).

Now feed the auger down through the overflow and into the trap. Cranking the auger all the way through the trap usually will clear the drain. If not, you'll have to remove the trap or a cleanout plug at its lowermost point, and auger toward the main drain. With a second-floor tub, this may involve making a hole in the ceiling below.

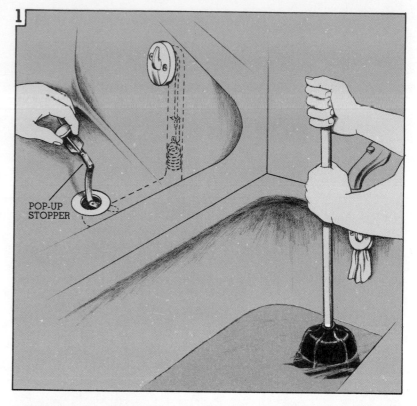

POP-UP STOPPER

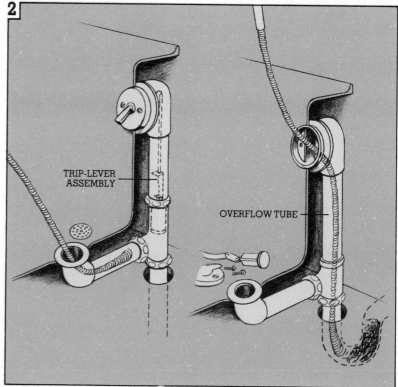

TRIP-LEVER ASSEMBLY

OVERFLOW TUBE

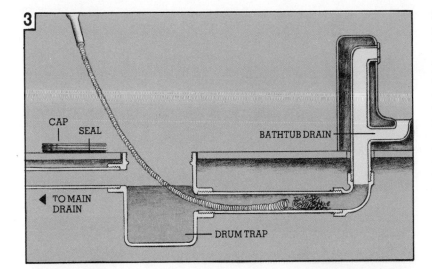

3 If there's a removable metal cap in the floor beside your tub, your tub is equipped with a *drum trap.* To free up one of these, begin by bailing out the tub; use rags or old towels to soak up any remaining water. Neglect to do this and the trap could flood over when you remove the cap.

Loosen it slowly, watching for water welling up around the threads. If this happens, mop up as you go. After you've removed the cap and its rubber seal, work the auger away from the tub toward the main drain.

If, on the other hand, the trap is only partially full, as shown here, the obstruction is between the tub and trap, and you should auger toward the tub.

4 A clogged shower drain may respond to plunging. If not, remove its strainer, which may be secured to the drain opening by a screw in the center or snapped into place.

5 Now probe an auger down the drain and through its trap. If this doesn't work, you may be able to blast out the blockage with a hose. Pack rags around it, hold everything in place, then turn the water fully on and off a few times.

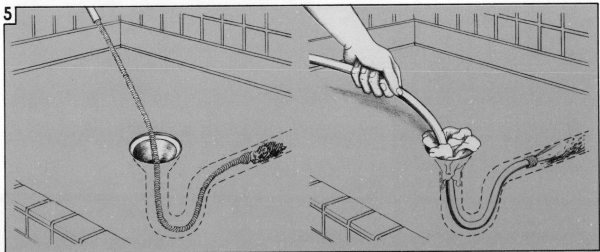

Opening Clogged Drains *(continued)*

Toilets

1 When a toilet clogs, don't flush it, or you'll also have a flood to deal with. Instead, use a bucket to carefully add or bail out water until the bowl is about half full. More than this could create a sloshy mess while you're plunging; too little, and the plunger won't make a tight seal around the bowl's outlet.

You can clear a toilet using an ordinary plunger, but the molded-cup type illustrated here generates stronger suction. Work up and down vigorously for about a dozen strokes, then yank away the plunger and observe the results.

If the water disappears with a glug, you probably have succeeded. Check by pouring in more water. You may need to repeat the process several more times. If it doesn't get results, try augering, as shown in sketch 2.

Note: Never attempt to unclog a toilet with a chemical drain cleaner. Chances are it won't do the job satisfactorily and you'll be forced to plunge or auger through a strong lye solution that could burn your skin or eyes.

2 A *closet auger* makes short work of most toilet stoppages. This specialized instrument has a longer handle than the trap-and-drain version that you'll find on preceding pages.

To operate it, pull the spring all the way up into the handle, insert the bit into the bowl outlet, and begin cranking. If you encounter resistance, pull back slightly, wiggle the handle, and try again.

A closet auger will chew out just about anything but a solid object, such as a toy or makeup jar. If you hear something other than the auger rattling around in there, you'll have to unscrew the hold-down nuts, pull up the bowl, turn it over, and shake or poke out the item.

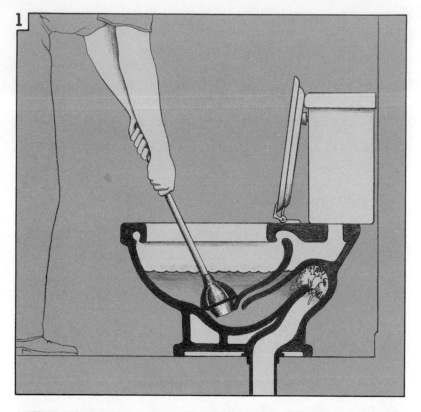

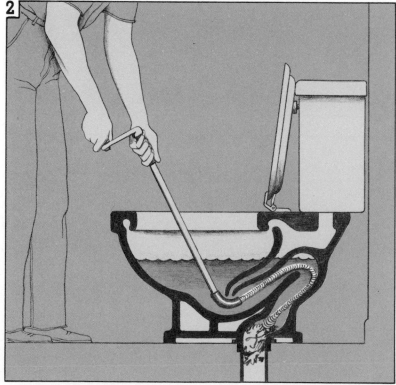

Main Drains and Sewer Lines

1 When one of these clogs, you may prefer to call in a plumber or drain-cleaning service. The work can be messy (you'll be dealing with raw sewage), and you may need a longer and stronger auger than the ones commonly used for fixture drains.

The key to getting an auger into a main drain is a Y-shaped fitting that is called a *cleanout*. You'll find one near the bottom of your home's soil stack, and there may be others higher up.

Begin by loosening the plug of that lowermost cleanout. If water oozes out, you can be sure the blockage is below somewhere. If not, try to find another cleanout above and work from there. Or climb up on the roof and auger down through the vent stack.

Before removing any cleanout, have buckets on hand to catch the waste water in the drain line.

Now thread an auger into the opening; work it back and forth a few times. Another often-successful way to clear main drains is to use a "blow bag" like the one illustrated.

2 If these procedures don't work, you'll have to move downstream.

Some houses have a house trap near where the drain lines leave the house. If your house does, open one of the trap plugs and thread in an auger. The blockage may be in the trap itself.

3 To clear a sewer line, try flushing it with a garden hose. Don't let the water run more than a minute or so, however; it could back up and cause drains to overflow. If this doesn't work, either contact a firm that specializes in opening clogged sewer lines or rent a *power auger.* Operating one of these is a two-person job.

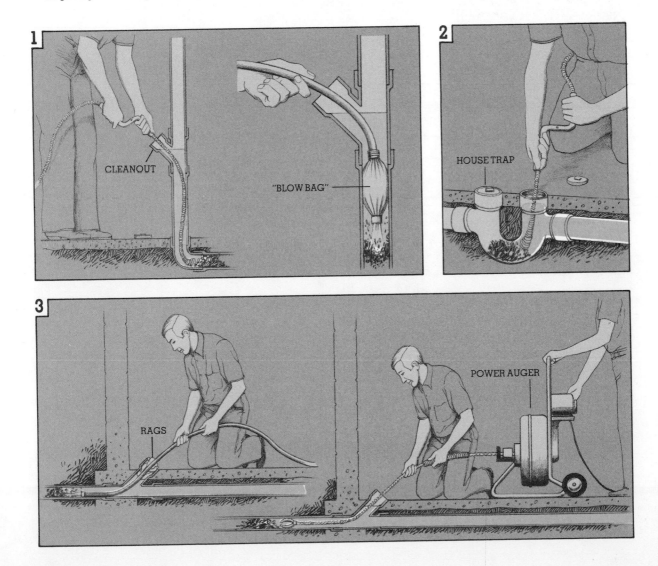

Dismantling Fixture Traps

Sometimes the plunging and augering techniques shown on pages 68-69 fail to clear a drain. Or perhaps you have dropped something into the drain and want to retrieve it. If either situation occurs, see whether the fixture's trap has a nutlike cleanout fitting at its bottommost point. Opening it lets you work an auger farther back toward the main drain or retrieve objects that have fallen in.

No cleanout? Don't be discouraged. It takes only a little more time and effort to remove the entire trap.

Trap configurations vary, but all include some combination of the slip-joint fittings shown below. These come apart and reassemble with only light wrench work.

1 Before you begin, shut off water at the fixture stops (or the system shutoff) or remove faucet knobs so no one can inadvertently flood the scene below. Position a bucket to catch water that will spill out when you remove the trap.

Now loosen any *slip nuts* securing the trap. Protect plating by wrapping tape around the jaws of your wrench or pliers. After a half-turn or so, you can unscrew the nuts by hand.

The exploded view here shows how *adjustable traps* dismantle. A *tailpiece* from the fixture slips into one end, an *elbow* connects the other end to a *drainpipe*. Most slip connections seal by compressing rubber washers; older ones may be packed instead with a stringlike lampwick for a tight seal. Other traps (not shown here) resemble Js and Ss. They also come apart.

2 *Fixed traps* have slip fittings only at one end. To disconnect one of these, loosen both slip nuts, slide the tailpiece into the trap, then turn the trap loose from the drainpipe.

Before you reassemble a slip fitting, check the washer for wear. Lampwick always should be replaced; wrap a couple of turns around before you begin threading on the nut.

Be careful, too, that you don't strip or overtighten a slip nut. Turn it as far as you can by hand, then use pliers or a wrench to go an additional quarter-revolution.

To test for leaks, completely fill the fixture, then open the drain and look over all connections. Slightly tighten any that leak.

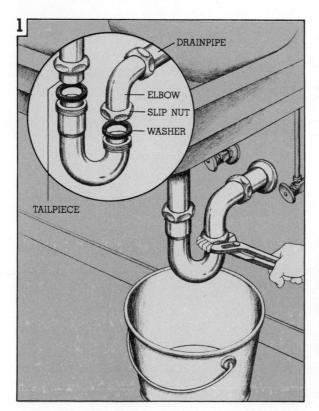

1 — DRAINPIPE / ELBOW / SLIP NUT / WASHER / TAILPIECE

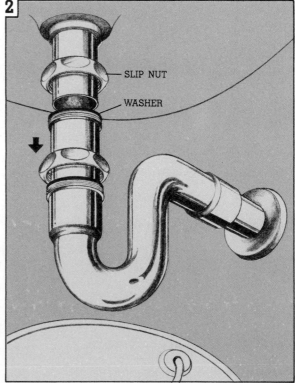

2 — SLIP NUT / WASHER

Adjusting Drain Assemblies

When water in a lavatory or tub pulls a disappearing act or the fixture seems to take forever emptying itself, be fairly certain that a pop-up or trip-lever assembly isn't doing its job properly. With just a pair of pliers and a screwdriver, you can put a stop to either problem quickly.

1 If your tub or lavatory has a *pop-up* mechanism similar to those illustrated in the sketches, first pull out the stopper and thoroughly clean away any hair, soap, or other matter that may be keeping it from seating snugly. (See page 67 for more information on removing lavatory stoppers.)

Next, check the *stopper seal*. If it's cracked or broken, pry off the rubber ring and install a new one. Look, too, for signs of wear or damage around the *flange* the stopper seats into.

Now replace the stopper and observe whether you can snug it down with the pop-up mechanism. If not, or if water is draining slowly, you need to make a simple adjustment or two.

For a lavatory, crouch under the basin and examine the position of the *pivot rod*. When the stopper is closed, this should slope slightly uphill from the *pivot* to the *clevis*. If it doesn't, loosen the setscrew, raise or lower the clevis on the *lift rod*, and retighten the screw.

Now the stopper may not operate as easily as it did before. You can adjust this by squeezing the *spring clip*, pulling the pivot rod out of the clevis, and reinserting it in the next higher or lower hole.

If water drips from the pivot, try giving its *cap* a turn to tighten it. Or you may need to replace the *pivot seal* inside.

To adjust a tub pop-in, unscrew the *overflow plate*, withdraw the entire assembly, and loosen the *adjusting nuts*. If the stopper doesn't seat tightly, move the *middle link* higher on the *striker rod*; if the tub is slow to drain, lower the link.

2 A *trip-lever* mechanism lifts and lowers a *seal plug* at the base of the overflow tube. When this drops into its *seat*, water from the tub drain can't get past. But because the plug is hollow, the overflow route is only slightly constricted.

Dismantle and adjust a trip-lever as you would a pop-up. Also check the *seal* on the bottom of the plug and replace it, if necessary.

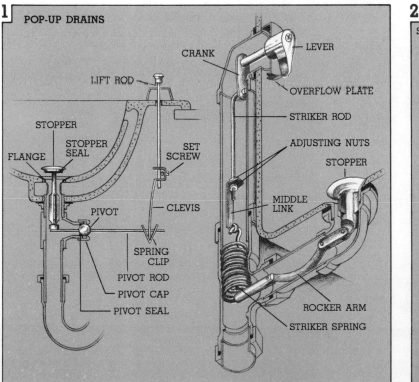

1 POP-UP DRAINS

LIFT ROD
CRANK
LEVER
STOPPER
STOPPER SEAL
FLANGE
SET SCREW
OVERFLOW PLATE
STRIKER ROD
ADJUSTING NUTS
STOPPER
MIDDLE LINK
PIVOT
CLEVIS
SPRING CLIP
PIVOT ROD
PIVOT CAP
PIVOT SEAL
ROCKER ARM
STRIKER SPRING

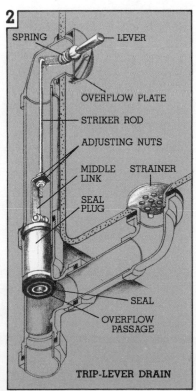

2
SPRING
LEVER
OVERFLOW PLATE
STRIKER ROD
ADJUSTING NUTS
MIDDLE LINK
STRAINER
SEAL PLUG
SEAL
OVERFLOW PASSAGE

TRIP-LEVER DRAIN

Repairing Leaky Faucets

A faucet's job is to deliver a stream of water on command, and rarely will yours fail to oblige whenever called upon. If trouble develops, it almost invariably results in a "drip, drip, drip" from the spout or causes an oozing around the body of the faucet.

If either of these problems crops up around your house, you first must identify what type of faucet you're dealing with, then repair or replace the faulty part. Start by looking over the anatomy drawings shown here and on the following pages.

Stem Faucets

Stem faucets, such as the ones below, always have separate hot and cold controls. With many types, turning a handle twists a threaded *stem* up or down. In its off position, the stem compresses a rubber-like *washer* into a beveled *seat,* stopping the flow of water. As the washer wears, you have to apply more and more pressure to turn off the unit. That's when dripping begins.

Newer w*asherless stem faucets* replace the washer with a much more durable *seal/-spring assembly.* With this type, the stem rotates rather than raising and lowering to control water flow.

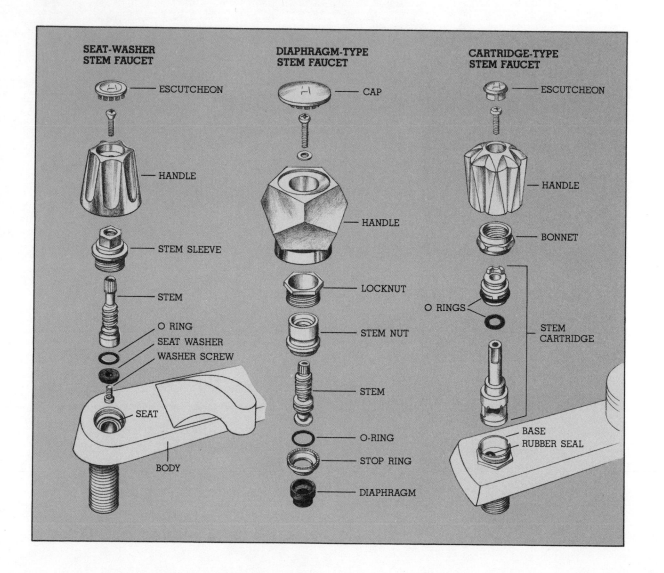

SEAT-WASHER STEM FAUCET — ESCUTCHEON, HANDLE, STEM SLEEVE, STEM, O RING, SEAT WASHER, WASHER SCREW, SEAT, BODY

DIAPHRAGM-TYPE STEM FAUCET — CAP, HANDLE, LOCKNUT, STEM NUT, STEM, O-RING, STOP RING, DIAPHRAGM

CARTRIDGE-TYPE STEM FAUCET — ESCUTCHEON, HANDLE, BONNET, O RINGS, STEM CARTRIDGE, BASE, RUBBER SEAL

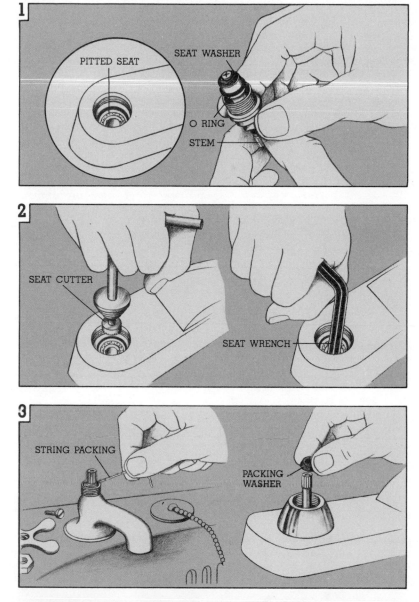

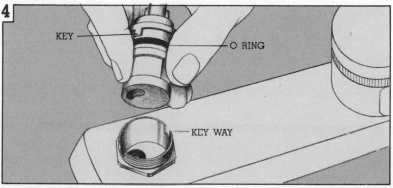

1 When the spout of a *threaded* stem faucet leaks, you can be sure that either the seat washer or the seat itself needs attention. Shut off the water supply to the faucet, then disassemble the faucet to the point where you can get a look at the washer at the base of the stem (see the anatomy drawing on the opposite page).

If the washer appears cracked, grooved, or partially missing, back out the screw holding the washer to the stem and insert a new washer. Also check the O ring around the stem as well as the packing or packing washer. Replace these if needed.

Maybe the washer isn't the troublemaker. The seat at the base of the faucet body may be pitted or badly corroded.

2 Depending on its condition, the seat may require either grinding or replacement. Special tools, a *seat cutter* and a *seat wrench,* perform these tasks. If you run up against a stubborn seat, squirt on some penetrating oil to free things up.

3 You usually can trace leaks around faucet handles and from the base of the faucet to O rings or stem packing. Both wear out eventually and should be replaced. Many older faucet stems came with packing that forms a tight seal under pressure. When replacing old packing, be sure to wrap the new packing clockwise around the stem. With newer faucets, a packing washer takes the place of the packing string.

4 If yours is the newer, cartridge-type stem like the one shown, it's best to replace the seal and O rings whenever the faucet acts up. Remove the seal and spring with the end of a pencil. When reinserting the cartridge, be sure to align the *key* with the *key way.*

Repairing Leaky Faucets *(continued)*

Tipping-Valve Faucets

Its slim *control handle* makes a tipping-valve faucet easy to identify. This handle connects to a *control cam*, which, when rotated, activates the two *tipping-valve mechanisms* under the body cover. These mechanisms have several components: a *plug, gasket, stem, spring, screen,* and *seat.*

Raising the faucet handle forces the cam against the valve stems, lifting them off their seat. The farther back you throw the handle, the more water that enters the mixing chamber.

Note the handle's position in the sketch below. At left of center, it rotates the cam to tip the hot water stem, allowing only a stream of hot water to pass through. The cold water stem remains unaffected.

For the most part, tipping-valve faucet troubles—all easy to spot and correct—originate in three areas.

Leaks from the spout portend a breakdown of one or more of the valve mechanism components. Fix these by replacing the whole mechanism. If you notice leakage around the handle, the cam assembly O ring has given way. Sketch 3 on page 79 shows how to repair this. Finally, leaks around the spout mean a bad spout O ring.

Although tipping-valve faucets no longer are made, you can still get the parts—usually sold in kit form—necessary to remedy all of these problems. The repair kit won't include a screen; it is no longer considered needed.

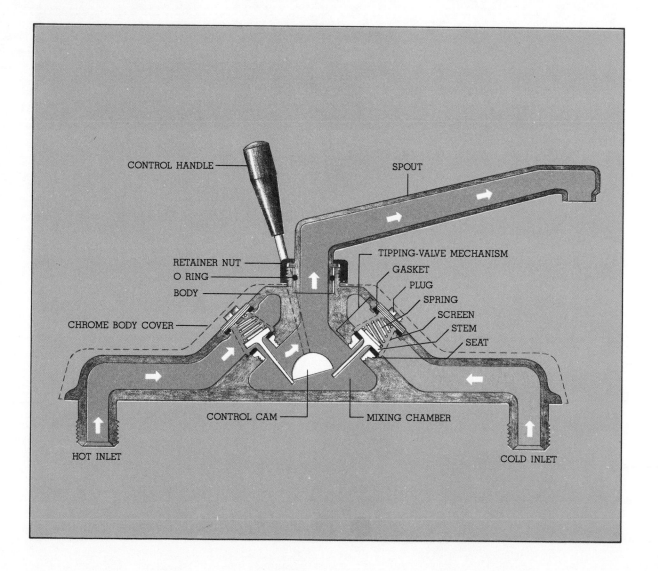

CONTROL HANDLE

SPOUT

RETAINER NUT

O RING

BODY

CHROME BODY COVER

TIPPING-VALVE MECHANISM

GASKET

PLUG

SPRING

SCREEN

STEM

SEAT

HOT INLET

CONTROL CAM

MIXING CHAMBER

COLD INLET

1 First things first. Shut off the water supply to the fixture and drain the water that remains at the faucet by raising the handle in its center position. To disassemble, loosen the retainer nut with a cloth-covered pair of pliers.

Next, grab hold of the spout and raise it out of the faucet body. If you spy a badly worn O ring, replace it with a new one.

2 To get the cam assembly, you'll need to loosen the setscrew holding the handle to the cam. The next step is to remove the rear closure that conceals the cam. Then remove the screws that hold the cam in place and pull the cam out of the faucet body. Set the cam aside. Lift off the body cover.

3 With the aid of a wrench, remove the valve assembly plug, then the screen, gasket, spring, stem, and the seat. (You'll need an allen wrench or a seat wrench to remove the seat.) Replace the entire assembly with the repair parts. Do the same with the other valve.

4 After making all of the above repairs, you'll have one O ring left for the cam assembly. Simply remove the old O ring and replace it with the new. You would do well to lubricate the new one to make it easier to replace the cam in the faucet body.

If your faucet has a spray attachment that has been acting up, now is a good time to check on the condition of the diverter valve. It's under the spout in the faucet body and can be best removed using a screwdriver and pliers. Clean its openings with a toothbrush. If this doesn't help, buy a new one. When shopping for a diverter, be sure to take the old one with you so your supplier can tell which type you have.

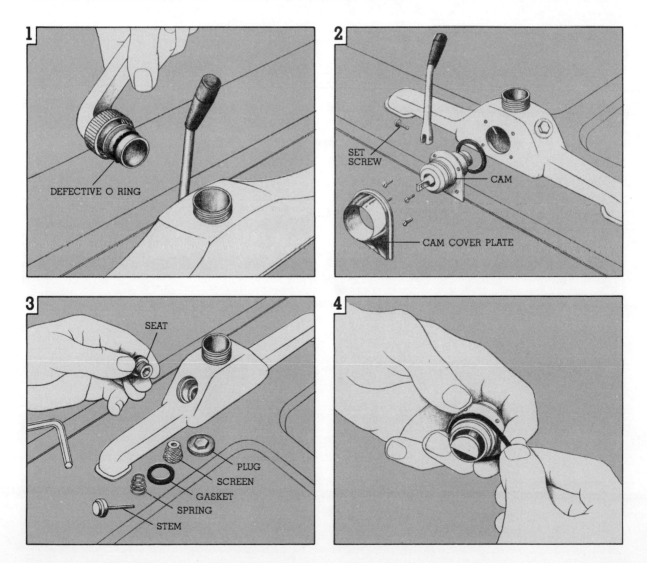

Repairing Leaky Faucets *(continued)*

Disc Faucets

As you can see by looking at the anatomy drawing below, disc faucets depend not on a washer and seat to shut off and control the flow of water, but on a *disc* arrangement.

Raising the faucet lever of one of these causes the upper portion of the disc assembly to slide across its lower half, allowing water to enter the *mixing chamber.* Naturally,

the higher you raise the lever, the more water you allow to enter the chamber. Conversely, lowering the lever closes off the *inlet ports.*

Moving the lever from side to side tells whether hot or cold water or a mixture of the two comes out of the spout.

The disc assembly itself, generally ceramic, rarely needs replacing. However, the inlet ports can become restricted by mineral deposits. If this happens, disassemble the faucet as shown opposite and scrape away the minerals with a pocketknife.

If the faucet leaks around its base, one or more of the *inlet seals* most likely needs replacing. It's a good idea to replace all of the seals because the failure of one usually signals the impending demise of the rest.

Most plumbing supply outlets stock repair kits for this as well as other types of faucets. Before going to your supplier for a replacement kit, jot down the brand of faucet you have (the name is on the faucet body). Or take the disc along if you already have removed it.

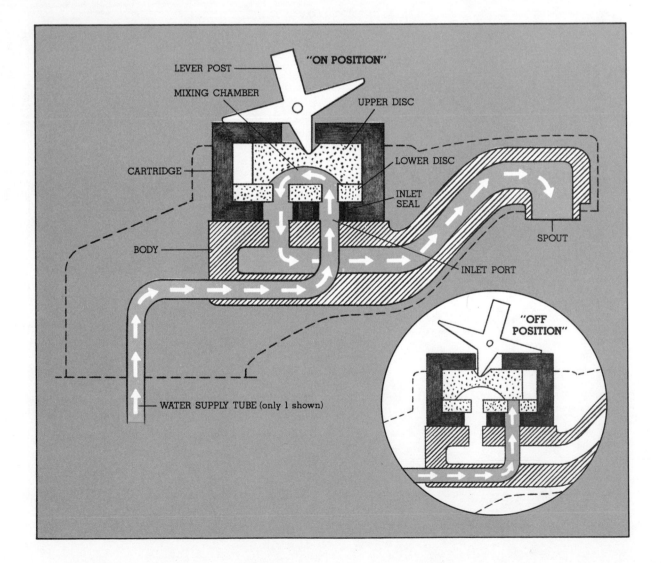

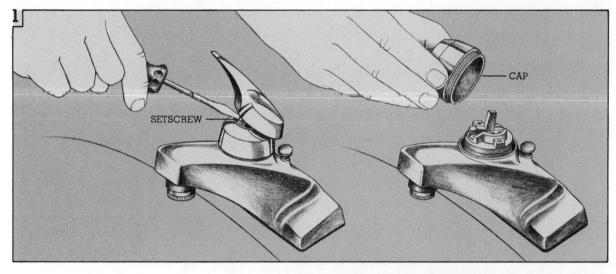

SETSCREW

CAP

1 To repair a leaky disc faucet, first shut off the water supply to the unit, then drain the lines by lifting the lever to its highest position. Look closely under the lever, and you'll see a setscrew that secures the lever to the lever post. Using an appropriately sized screwdriver, turn the setscrew counterclockwise until you can raise the lever off the post.

Next, lift off or unscrew the decorative cap that conceals the cartridge. With this out of the way, loosen the screws holding the cartridge to the faucet body, then lift out the cartridge.

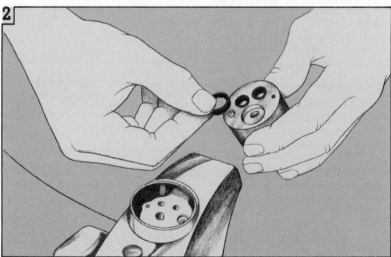

2 On the underside of the cartridge you'll find a set of seals. To replace them, just pull out the old, worn ones and insert the new. While you're doing this, check for sediment buildup around the inlet ports, and thoroughly remove it to clear the restriction.

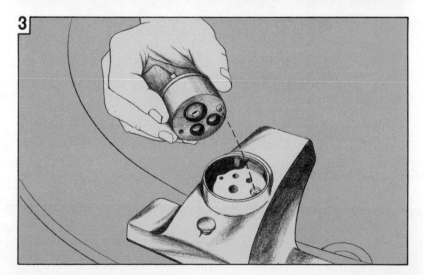

3 Reassemble the faucet, reversing the disassembly procedures. When inserting the cartridge, be sure to align its holes with those in the base of the faucet body.

Repairing Leaky Faucets *(continued)*

Rotating-Ball Faucets

Inside every rotating-ball faucet, a slotted *ball* sits atop a pair of spring-loaded rubber seals. In the "off" position, this ball (held tight against the seals by the cap) closes off the supply of water.

But look what happens when the faucet handle is raised (see detail drawings). The ball rotates in such a way that its openings begin to align with the supply line ports. When this happens, water can pass through the ball and on out the spout. Moving the handle to the left allows more hot water into the mixing chamber, while moving it to the right provides more cold water.

Not surprisingly, the seals and springs can give out, usually after long use. You'll find out how to replace these on page 83.

Realize, too, that these faucets can spring leaks from around the handle and, in swivel-spout models, from under the base of the spout. Handle leaks indicate that either the *adjusting ring* has loosened a bit or the *seal* immediately above the ball has worn.

Under-spout leaks, on the other hand, result from O-ring failure. Inspect the rings encircling the *body*. On units with diverter valves, inspect the valve's O ring as well. Replace it, if necessary, as shown opposite.

While you have the faucet apart, check the ball for wear and corrosion. If it's faulty, replace it with a new one.

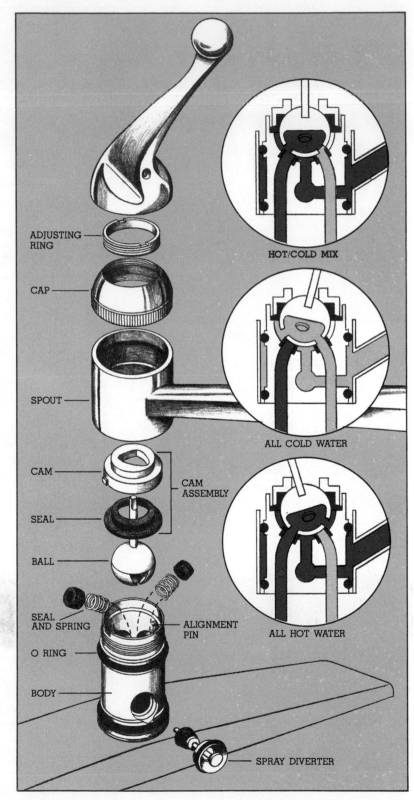

ADJUSTING RING

CAP

SPOUT

CAM

CAM ASSEMBLY

SEAL

BALL

SEAL AND SPRING

ALIGNMENT PIN

O RING

BODY

SPRAY DIVERTER

HOT/COLD MIX

ALL COLD WATER

ALL HOT WATER

1 To disassemble a rotating-ball faucet, first shut off the water supply, then drain the lines by lifting straight up on the handle. Using an allen wrench, loosen the setscrew holding the handle in place.

Next, loosen the adjusting ring (the wrench packed with repair kits is the correct tool), and unscrew the cap. You may need to apply pressure with cloth-covered adjustable pliers to budge the cap.

2 Lift out the cam assembly, ball, and, in the case of a swivel-spout faucet, the spout. The spout, being friction-fit around the body, may prove to be stubborn. So be pre-pared to apply some muscle at this point (but not so much that you weaken the plumbing below).

On the other hand, to remove worn seals and springs from the body requires only minimal effort. Simply insert either end of a lead pencil into each seat, then withdraw the pencil. Check for restriction at the supply inlet ports, scrape away any buildup you find, then insert the new springs and seals.

3 If the faucet has a swivel-spout, pry the O rings away from the body using a sharp-pointed tool. Roll the new ones down over the body until they rest in the appropri-ate grooves. Replace the diverter O ring in the same manner.

4 As you reassemble the faucet, be aware that you must align the slot in the side of the ball with the pin inside the body. Also note that the key on the cam assembly fits into a corresponding notch in the body of the faucet.

After hand-tightening the cap, tighten the adjusting ring for a good seal between the ball and cam. If there is a leak around the handle after restoring pressure to the lines, carefully tighten the adjusting ring a bit more.

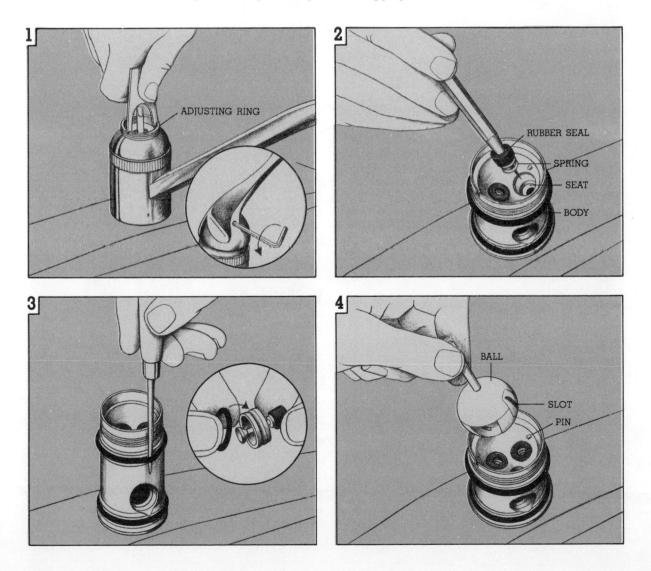

Repairing Leaky Faucets (continued)

Sleeve-Cartridge Faucets

Most washerless faucets rely on a combination of seals and O rings to control and direct water. Not so with the sleeve-cartridge type. Instead, the cartridge itself is ringed by a series of strategically placed O rings.

Look at the anatomy drawing below and you can see that the O rings fit snugly against the inside of the faucet body. This arrangement serves two purposes. The diagonally set O ring forms a seal between the hot and cold supply lines. The other O rings ensure against leaks from the spout, from under the handle, and from under the spout on swivel-spout models.

Note, too, that when the handle is raised, the stem also raises and the holes in it align with the openings in the cartridge. You control the temperature by rotating the handle to the left or the right.

When this type of faucet acts up, you can replace either the O rings or the cartridge itself if it has corroded. And because of the faucet's simple design and few replaceable parts, repairing one generally doesn't take long. In fact, disassembling the faucet may account for the bulk of the work involved. Both of these procedures are covered on page 83.

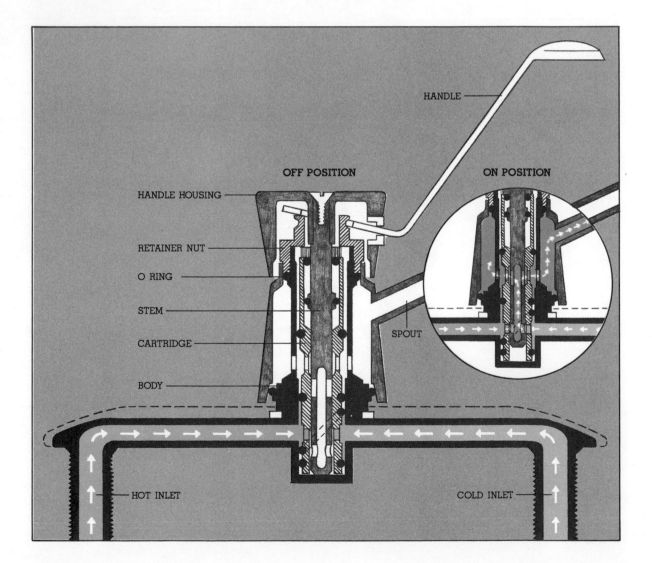

HANDLE

OFF POSITION   ON POSITION

HANDLE HOUSING

RETAINER NUT

O RING

STEM

CARTRIDGE

BODY

SPOUT

HOT INLET   COLD INLET

1 Sleeve-cartridge faucets vary somewhat in design from model to model, but all disassemble pretty much as follows. As always, you must shut off and drain the water lines first.

With that out of the way, pry off the decorative handle cover concealing the handle screw. Be careful not to crack the cover in doing so; most are made of plastic.

Now remove the handle screw and lift off the handle assembly. On swivel-spout models, you'll encounter a *retainer nut.* Unscrew it, then lift off the spout.

Depending on the model you have, you may need to lift off a cy-lindrical sleeve to get at the cartridge. You should now be able to see the *retainer clip,* the device that holds the cartridge in place. Using long-nose pliers, remove the clip from its slot.

2 With pliers, lift the cartridge from the faucet body. Note the position of the *cartridge ears.* They face the front and back of the faucet, and it's important that when the cartridge is replaced they be in exactly the same position.

3 Remove the O rings, install new ones, and reinsert the cartridge and retainer clip. If yours is a swiv-el-spout model, lubricate the O rings around the outside of the body, then force the spout down over the rings and into position.

4 Tighten the retaining nut, using adhesive-bandaged or cloth-coated pliers to guard against marring the chrome spout. Finish the job by reinstalling the handle, restoring water pressure, and checking the faucet for leaks.

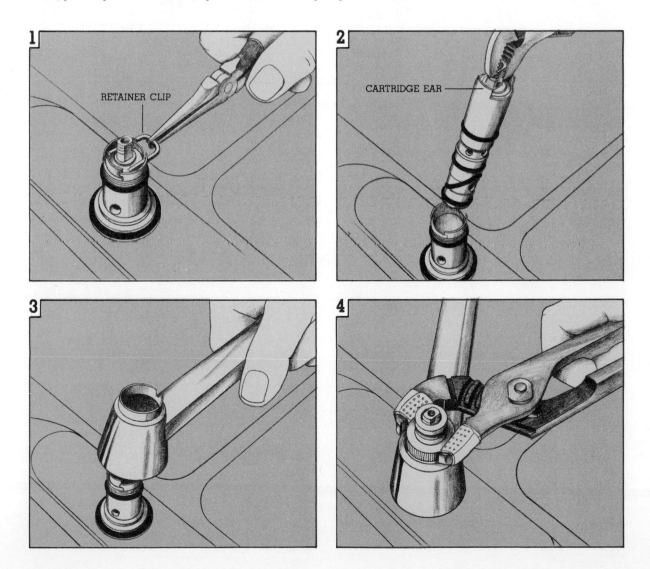

Repairing Sink Sprays, Diverters, Aerators

As mentioned earlier, some sink and lavatory faucets have sprays and diverter valves. And most all have an aerator at the tip of the spout. With sprays, troubles can develop in the connections, gaskets, or the nozzle. Most often, you can trace diverter maladies to worn washers or O rings. And about the only troubles that crop up with aerators are leaks caused by a worn gasket or a loose housing, and "low pressure" that results from mineral deposits clogging the screen. Fortunately, however, you can troubleshoot and correct all of these problems with a minimum of hassles.

1 Although diverters vary in shape from brand to brand, all operate in much the same way as the one shown here. When water isn't flowing toward the spray outlet, the valve remains open and allows water to proceed out the spout. But notice how it reacts when you press the nozzle lever. It closes off the passage leading to the spout.

If nothing happens when you press the lever, check to see whether the hose is kinked. A slow stream of water coupled with some water coming from the spout may signal a stuck valve or a worn washer or O ring. (See step 2). To check out the diverter, disassemble the faucet (see pages 78-85 for help with this). You'll find the diverter in the faucet body under the spout or in the spout itself. Replace faulty parts or the diverter itself, if needed.

2 Minerals may be restricting the flow of water through the spray. Clean the spray disc with a straight pin as shown. Check other parts of the spray for wear and tighten all connections.

3 To check out a suspect aerator, disassemble it, then brush the screen clean if necessary.

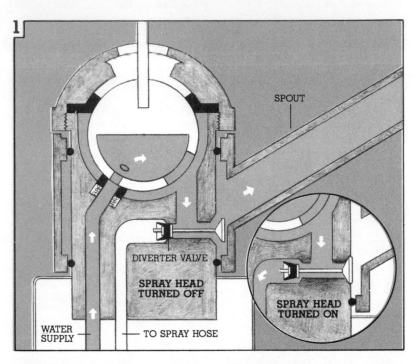

SPOUT

DIVERTER VALVE

SPRAY HEAD TURNED OFF

SPRAY HEAD TURNED ON

WATER SUPPLY

TO SPRAY HOSE

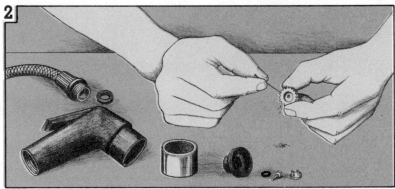

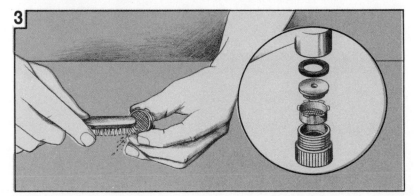

Repairing Tub/Shower Diverters

Tub/shower diverters fall into two general classifications. Those of one group, typified by the stem-type valve in the upper portion of the sketch, are housed in the faucet body and direct the flow of water from there. Tub diverter spouts, on the other hand, act independently of the faucet.

The sketch at right shows how each works. In the closed position, the diverter valve blocks off the water flow to the shower head. Opened fully, it diverts incoming water to the shower head. Diverter mechanisms vary by manufacturer, but they all do the same thing.

With the tub diverter spout shown, lifting up on its knob while the water is running seals off the inlet to the spout and forces the water up to and out of the shower head. The water pressure will maintain the seal. When the water is shut off the knob will drop back into its usual position.

When a tub diverter spout wears out, or if the lift rod attached to the knob breaks off from the plate it is attached to, you may as well replace the spout. To remove the defective one, insert a hammer handle or another suitable item into the spout and rotate it counterclockwise until it separates from the nipple it is attached to. Wrap pipe compound or tape around the nipple and install the new spout.

If a stem-type valve begins to leak or no longer will divert water properly, shut off the water supply to the faucet, drain the lines, and remove the nut holding the stem in place. Withdraw the stem, inspect the packing washer or O ring and the seat washer if your diverter has one, and replace any worn-out parts you find.

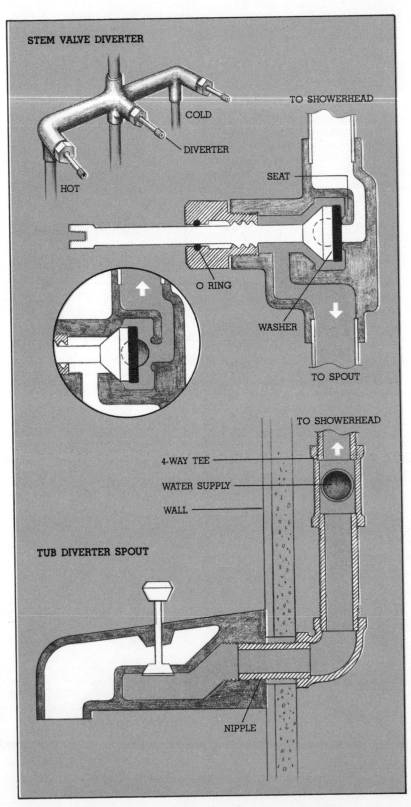

STEM VALVE DIVERTER

COLD

TO SHOWERHEAD

DIVERTER

SEAT

HOT

O RING

WASHER

TO SPOUT

TO SHOWERHEAD

4-WAY TEE

WATER SUPPLY

WALL

TUB DIVERTER SPOUT

NIPPLE

Repairing Toilets

Ever had to fiddle endlessly with the flush handle of a toilet to stop the water? Or fight with a tank ball that just refuses to rest squarely in its seat? Or peer helplessly into a toilet tank wondering what on earth is causing that incessant trickle of water? You're not alone.

Most people could care less about how toilets do what they do. But the sad fact is that someday you're going to have to become acquainted with this necessary household unit. Let's take a behind-the-scenes look at a typical toilet and its rather simple inner workings.

When someone flips the *flush handle,* a chain-reaction occurs. The *trip lever* lifts up the *tank ball* via a *lift wire/ lift rod* arrangement. As the water rushes down through the *ball seat* and *flush passages* into the *bowl,* the reservoir of water and the waste in the bowl yield to gravity and pass through the toilet's *trap* out into a nearby drain line.

Inside the tank, the *float ball* rides the tide of the outrushing water until, at a predetermined level, the rod it attaches to trips the *flush valve.* (The tank ball settles back into its seat at this time, too.) This valve allows a new supply of water to enter the tank through a *fill tube* and the bowl through the *overflow tube.* When the float returns to its full position, the flush valve (or ball cock) closes, completing the process.

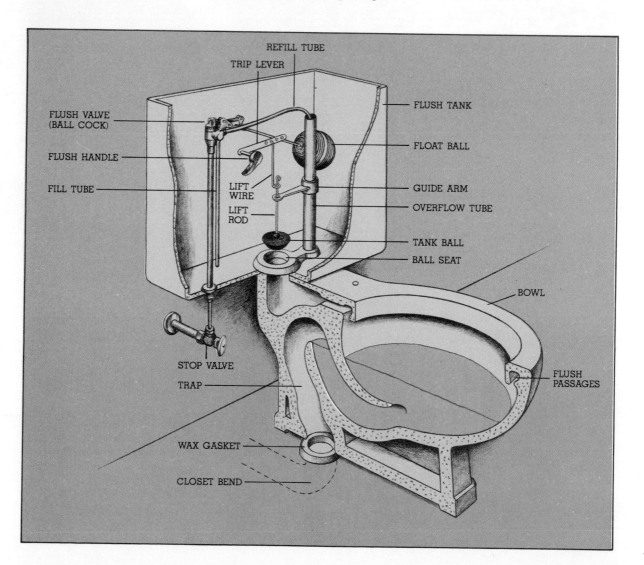

REFILL TUBE

TRIP LEVER

FLUSH VALVE (BALL COCK)

FLUSH HANDLE

FILL TUBE

LIFT WIRE

LIFT ROD

FLUSH TANK

FLOAT BALL

GUIDE ARM

OVERFLOW TUBE

TANK BALL

BALL SEAT

BOWL

FLUSH PASSAGES

STOP VALVE

TRAP

WAX GASKET

CLOSET BEND

Flush Tank Repairs

Because most of the mechanical action goes on inside the flush tank, it's not surprising that most problems develop there. Here's a rundown of some common maladies and their solutions.

1 If you have difficulty getting the flush valve to close after a flush, the *float rod* may not be raising up high enough. Remove the tank cover, being careful not to chip it, and lift the rod with your hand. If the flush valve closes, use two hands and bend the rod downward slightly. This simple procedure may solve the problem.

2 It's also possible the float ball has taken on some water. When this happens, the ball won't rise high enough to close the valve. To check out this possibility, agitate the ball and listen for a swishing sound. To remove a faulty ball, rotate it counterclockwise until you disengage it from the float rod. Replace the ball with a new one.

3 If the float ball passes inspection, look next at the flush valve (ball cock) assembly. **Before attempting to remove the float rod mechanism, however, shut off the water supply and flush the toilet.** Remove the thumbscrews holding the assembly in place, then lift it out and set it aside. (If yours is a diaphragm-type flush valve assembly, refer to the detail for help.)

4 Slip the blade of a screwdriver through the slot at the top of the plunger and lift it up out of the housing. Typically, you'll find a seat washer as well as one or more split washers. Remove and replace all of the washers, reassemble the flush valve assembly, and restore water pressure.

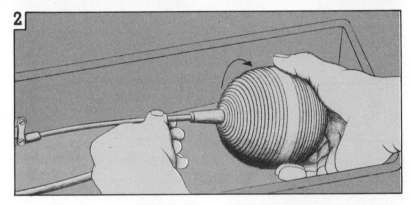

1 FLOAT BALL

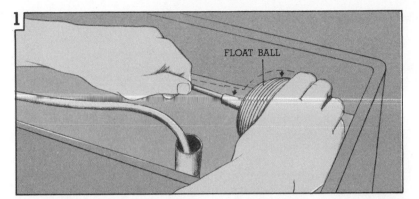

2

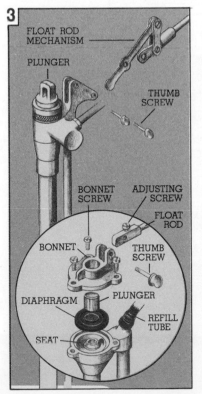

3 FLOAT ROD MECHANISM — PLUNGER — THUMB SCREW — BONNET SCREW — ADJUSTING SCREW — FLOAT ROD — BONNET — THUMB SCREW — PLUNGER — DIAPHRAGM — REFILL TUBE — SEAT

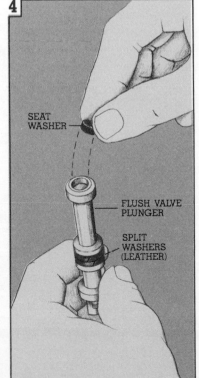

4 SEAT WASHER — FLUSH VALVE PLUNGER — SPLIT WASHERS (LEATHER)

Flush Tank Repairs *(cont.)*

5 Of course, if for some reason water continues to leak out of the tank, the valve controlling incoming water may never get a chance to shut off. Or it may shut off only temporarily. If either situation fits your circumstance, and the float ball and flush valve check out properly, you most likely have *tank ball* or *ball seat* problems.

Start by observing the tank ball as the tank empties. Does it settle squarely in its seat? If not, loosen the *guide arm* and rotate it for better alignment. Also check the *lift wire/lift rod* assembly and bend ei-

ther part, if necessary, so the ball seats properly.

6 If the tank ball needs replacing, unscrew it from the lift rod and install a new one. Or, to eliminate any future problems with the lift wire, lift rod, or guide arm, replace the old ball with a *flapper* and chain. To do this, disengage the lift wire from the trip arm, then loosen and lift out the guide arm. Slip the flapper down over the overflow tube and fasten the chain to the trip-lever mechanism.

7 A pitted or otherwise corroded ball seat also can prevent the tank

from filling properly. To check out the seat, run your finger completely around it. If you detect a problem, scour the seat with a steel wool pad to remove rough spots.

8 Newer flush valve assemblies, such as the one shown, simplify the flushing operation. And because they're corrosion-resistant plastic, they seldom act up. Sliding the float cup up or down on the rod permits you to control the level of water in the tank.

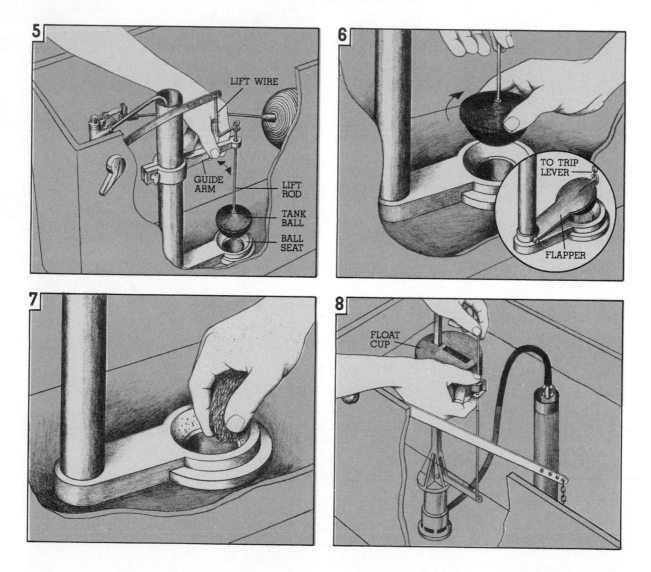

Stopping Exterior Leaks

1 As you can see, a *beveled gasket* at the base of the flushing valve shank and a *rubber washer* immediately beneath the tank (under pressure from a *locknut*) form a tight seal between the water inside the tank and the outside. Over time, however, either the locknut can work loose or the seals can give out.

If you notice a leak here, first tighten the locknut. If that doesn't work, shut off the water supply, flush the toilet, and sponge out the water that remains in the tank. Disconnect the water supply line, remove the locknut holding the flush valve assembly in place, and replace the old gasket and washer with new ones. Also, check the supply line washer for wear and replace it, if necessary.

2 Extended use also can cause the *tank hold-down bolts* to loosen just enough to produce a leak. Solving this problem is not difficult. Use a wrench and a long-shanked screwdriver to snug down the bolt as shown here.

3 With some older toilets, the tank connects to the bowl via a fitting similar to the one shown. If leaks develop at either end of the fitting, tightening the nuts should dry things up in a hurry.

4 Leaks from around the base of the bowl indicate one of three things. The *bowl hold-down bolts* may need tightening, the *wax gasket* around the bowl inlet needs replacing, or the bowl is cracked.

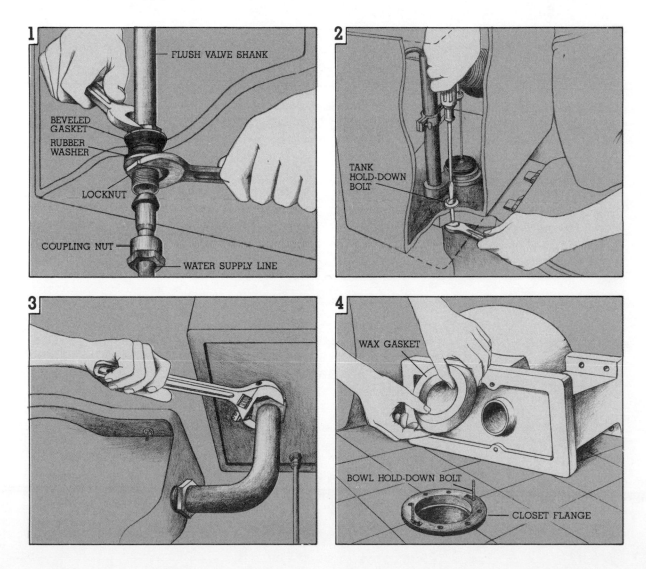

Troubleshooting Food Waste Disposers

A loud clanking noise, the strained buzz of an electric motor, or no action at all—any of these symptoms means you have waste disposer probems. Fortunately, the symptom often is worse than the illness. And if you know how to diagnose these strange goings-on, you should be able to get things going again without the expense of a plumber or a time-consuming trip to your plumbing parts supplier.

1 Disposers are pretty tough customers, but they're no match for flatware, bottle caps, and the like. If one of these undesirables accidentally falls into the grinding chamber, you'll hear the commotion right away. At best, the grinding blade will deform the item. Worse, a jam can result.

If your unit jams, shut off the power to it. Then remove the splashguard and survey the situation. Once you locate the obstruction, insert the end of a broom or mop handle into the grinding chamber and pry against the turntable until it rotates freely. With one brand of disposer, you insert an allen wrench into a hole in the bottom of the disposer, and work the tool back and forth. Remove the obstruction from the chamber. Impossible jams require professional attention.

2 If your disposer motor shuts off while in operation, its overload protector probably sensed overheating and broke electrical contact. To reactivate the motor, wait about five minutes for it to cool, then push the reset button (it's on the bottom of the disposer).

If the unit won't start, make sure the fuse or circuit breaker controlling the flow of power to the disposer is functioning. Verify, too, that the unit is plugged in or otherwise connected to the power source.

3 Since a disposer gobbles up huge amounts of food waste, it's only to be expected that occasionally the drain line may clog. If this happens, disassemble the trap (make sure you have a pan or bucket beneath it to catch the water that will spill).

If the trap itself is clear, thread a drain auger into the drainpipe.

Caution: Do not attempt to clear a blocked drain line with chemicals of any type because if the solution doesn't work, you'll have a line filled with caustic chemicals.

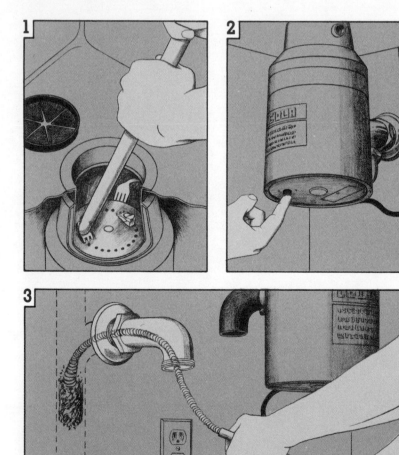

Quieting Noisy Pipes

Considering the conditions under which your home's water pipes operate, it's not surprising they make the noises they do. But that doesn't make their unexpected outbursts any less distracting. So if you've had it with that tick, tick, ticking, with the loud banging, and with all the other irritating clatter your pipes produce, read on.

Water hammer is perhaps the most common pipe noise of all. It results from a sudden stop in the flow of water, as would be the case when you turn off a fast-closing faucet.

You can usually trace ticking to a hot water pipe that was cool, then suddenly heated by circulating water.

Machine gun rattle, the annoying sound sometimes heard when you barely open a faucet, may indicate a seat washer is defective or loose. Air trapped in the water lines also can be the culprit.

1 Usually, you can guess at the vicinity of a noisy pipe just by listening. So begin your sleuthing by going to the basement and checking to see whether one of the pipes has been knocking up against or rubbing a floor joist or subflooring. Once you've found the trouble spot, simply cushioning the pipe as shown here may be all you need to do. Short lengths of rubber pipe insulation are ideal for this.

2 The only sure way to deal effectively with water hammer is to install *water shock arrestors*, or *air chambers*, at strategic locations in your water lines. As you can see here, there are several ways to go, but the goal is always the same: to provide a cushion of air for water to bang up against. Ideally, you should outfit each water supply line leading to each fixture with one of these devices. But to cut down on costs, start with those lines you know are causing problems. Installing a large air chamber between the water meter and the water heater makes good sense, too.

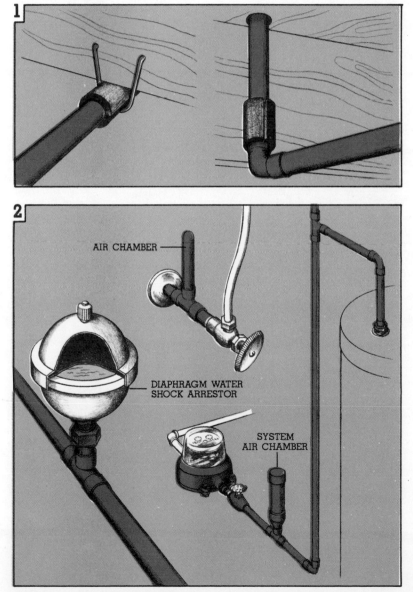

AIR CHAMBER

DIAPHRAGM WATER SHOCK ARRESTOR

SYSTEM AIR CHAMBER

Remedies for Leaky and Frozen Pipes

If you've ever had a plumbing emergency at your house, you already know that water on the loose can wreak havoc. Even a tiny leak left to drip day and night will soon rot away everything in its vicinity. A pipe that freezes and bursts can cause a major flood when the thaw comes.

As soon as you spot a leak, shut off the water to take pressure off the line. Then locate exactly where the prob-

lem lies. Water can run a considerable distance along the *outside* of a pipe, a floor joist, or the subfloor. That is why it may take time and a strong light to discover the source of the problem.

Ultimately, any leaking pipe or fitting will need replacing. Meanwhile, unless you're dealing with a gusher or the problem is buried in a wall, floor, or ceiling, the temporary measures shown here

will serve until you can make a permanent repair.

Left unattended, any frozen pipe will turn into a leaking one, so you'll want to take immediate action when a freeze-up occurs. Again, these remedies will get you through a crisis but not necessarily prevent a recurrence.

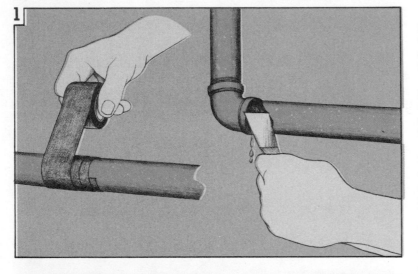

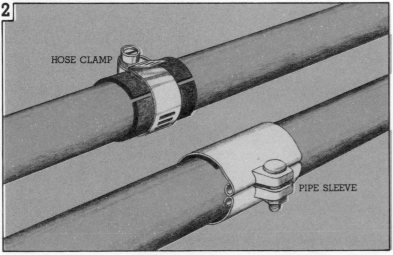

HOSE CLAMP

PIPE SLEEVE

1 For a pinhole leak, dry off the pipe and wrap it with several layers of plastic electrician's tape. Wind it about 6 inches in either direction of the hole.

At fittings, your best bet is to pack epoxy plumber's putty around the connection. This fast-setting compound makes a water-tight patch.

2 An automotive *hose clamp* and a piece of rubber, both available at automobile service stations, also make an effective leak stopper. Wrap the rubber around the pipe and tighten the clamp.

The galvanized pipe commonly used in homes built a generation ago tends to rust from the inside out. Once a leak appears, you can expect others to follow. If the pipes at your house have begun to deteriorate, lay in a supply of *pipe sleeves* sized to fit your lines. These make semipermanent repairs that will last for several years.

If a leak seems to be more a drip than a squirt, and you can't find where it's coming from, the pipe simply may be sweating. Wrapping it with insulation will eliminate condensation.

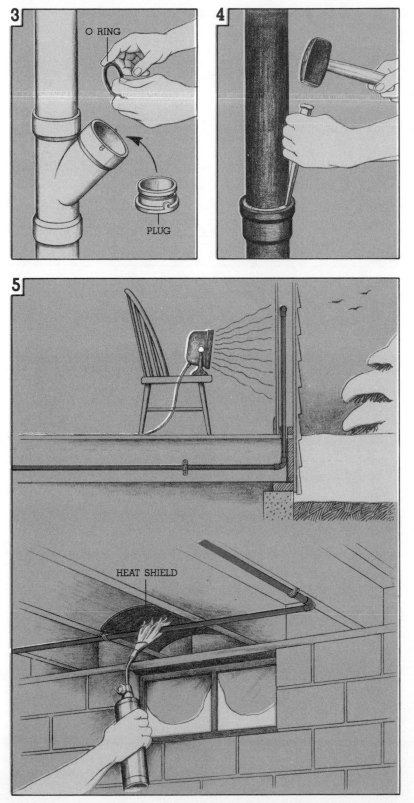

3 Drain-waste-vent (or DWV) lines are less prone to leak. Once in a while, however, a cleanout plug will begin to ooze water.

If this happens at your house, warn everyone not to use any fixtures for a few minutes, then remove the plug and reseal it. For iron plugs, wrap the threads with pipe tape or coat them with joint compound. Plastic plugs twist free. Lubricate the O ring with petroleum jelly and replace the plug.

4 Leaks at the joints of cast-iron DWV pipes are easy to deal with. If yours is the hub-and-spigot type illustrated here, tamping down the soft lead it has been sealed with usually will eliminate the problem. Don't whack the pipe too hard, though; you could crack it.

Or perhaps your home's DWV lines are connected with no-hub clamping system. If so, simply tightening the clamp probably will stop the leak.

5 Frozen pipes obviously need to be warmed, and how you apply the heat depends to some extent on where the pipe is. If it's concealed in a ceiling, wall, or floor, beam a heat lamp at the surface. Keep it 8 to 12 inches away so you don't risk starting a fire.

A propane torch offers the quickest (but riskiest) way to thaw exposed pipes. Never use one near gas lines, however, and use a heat shield to protect combustible materials. Ice tends to form along the entire length of a pipe, so put a spreader tip on the torch and move it back and forth. Don't let the pipe get too hot to touch; steam pressure could explode it.

If you don't have a torch or if the pipes are in tight quarters, wrap them with towels and pour hot water over the frozen section. Or heat the pipe with a hair drier. Regardless of how you choose to thaw out a pipe, first open the faucet it supplies so steam can escape.

Preventing Pipe Freeze-Ups

Icy-cold tap water may taste refreshing, but it's also a chilling omen that a pipe or pipes are in peril. Here are some steps you can take to bring them in from the cold.

1 Electric heat tape draws only modest amounts of current. You simply wrap it around the pipe and plug one end into an outlet. A thermostat turns the tape on and off as needed. Tape won't, of course, work during power outages, the times your home most needs protection against the freezing cold.

2 Pipe jacketing comes in standard lengths you cut with a knife and secure with plastic electrical tape. Ordinary insulation, cut in strips and bundled around pipes, works equally well. Be sure to insulate all joints and connections, too.

   In an extremely cold wall or floor, you may be better off to pack the entire cavity with insulation. Also consider insulating long hot-water runs, especially any that pass through unheated spaces. You'll conserve water-heating energy.

3 As an emergency preventive, crack open the faucet you're concerned about and let water trickle through the line. If there's a cabinet underneath, open its doors and let room heat warm the pipes. Beaming a small lamp at the pipes also protects short runs through cold spaces during winter's worst.

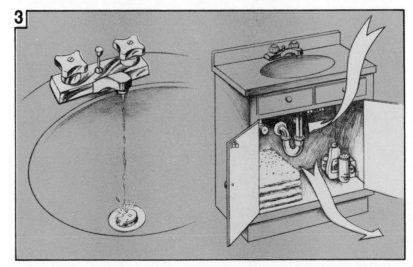

Index

A-B

Adjustable traps, 72
Aerators, sink, 84
Air chambers, installing, 91
Auger, drain, use of, 67, 68, 69, 70, 71
Ball seat problems, 88
Bathtubs. *See* Tubs
Brick pavers, cleaning, 28
Bypass doors, repair of, 47

C

Carpeting, repair of
  bubbles, removal of, 27
  replacement of damaged sections, 24-26
  seams, 26-27
  stain removal, 25
Cartridge fuses, 52, 53
Ceiling and wall repairs. *See* Wall and ceiling repairs
Ceramic tile
  floor, cleaning, 28
  wall, replacing, 16
Chimes, door, repairing, 64-65
Circuit breakers, tripped, 51
Cleanouts, 71
  resealing, 93
Clogged drains, opening, 67
  food waste disposers, 90
  main and sewer, 71
  sinks and lavatories, 67
  toilets, 70
  tubs and showers, 68-69
Closet auger, use of, 70
Concrete floors, repair of, 28
Continuity tester, 52, 61
Cords, electrical, 54, 57
Cracks, mending
  in concrete floors, 28
  in drywall, 9
  in plaster, 13-14
Crank-operated windows, repair of, 40-41
Cutting tools, 6

D-G

Disc faucets, 78-79
Disposers, food waste, 90
Diverters, 84
  tipping-valve faucet, 77
  tub/shower, 85
Door chimes, repairing, 64-65

Doors, repair of, 42-49
  garage, 48-49
  hinged, 43
    binding, freeing of, 43
    latch and strike plate, 45
    loose and squeaky hinges, 44
  sliding, 46
    bypass, 47
    patio, 46-47
Double-hung windows
  repairing
    freeing of sash, 37
    sash cord, replacing, 38
    spring-loaded balances, 39
  sills, 36
Drain-waste-vent (DWV) lines, leaks in, 93
Drains
  assemblies, adjusting, 73
  clogged, opening. *See* Clogged drains, opening
  traps, dismantling, 72
Drum trap, clearing, 69
Drywall surfaces, repairing, 9-12
DWV lines, leaks in, 93
Efflorescence, removal of, 28
Electric heat tape, 94
Electrical repairs, 50-65
  circuit breakers, 51
  cords, 54, 57
  door chimes, 64-65
  fluorescent fixtures, 62-63
  fuses, 52-53
  incandescent fixtures, 60
  plugs, 54, 55-56
  receptacles, 59
  sockets, lamp, 57
  switches, 58, 61
  tools for, 6
Faucets, repairing, 74
  disc, 78-79
  rotating-ball, 80-81
  sleeve-cartridge, 82-83
  sprays and diverters, 84
  stem, 74-75
  tipping-valve, 76-77
  tools for, 6
Floors, repair of, 18-29
  bubbles in carpet, 27
  carpeting, 25-27
  hard-surface, 28-29
  replacement of damaged sections
    carpeting, 25-26
    concrete, 28

  sheet goods, 24
  tiles, hard-surface, 29
  tiles, resilient, 23-24
  wood, 22
  resilient surface, 23-24
  scratches, hiding, 21
  seams, carpet, 26-27
  squeaks, silencing, 19-20
  stain removal
    carpeting, 25
    hard-surface flooring, 28
    wood, 21
  wood, 19-22
Fluorescent fixtures, 62-63
Flush tank repairs, 87-88
Food waste disposers, 90
Frozen pipes
  preventing, 94
  thawing, 93
Fuses, 52-53
Garage doors, repair of, 48-49
Grout
  removal of stains from, 28
  replacement, 16, 29

H-L

Hard-surface flooring repairs, 28-29
Heat tape, electric, 94
Heater plugs, 56
Hinged doors, repair of, 43
  binding, freeing of, 43
  latch and strike plate, 45
  loose and squeaky hinges, 44
Holes, patching
  in concrete floors, 28
  in drywall, 10-11
  in plaster, 13-14
  in screening, 31
Incandescent fixtures, 60
Insulation for pipes, 94
Joint compound, use of, 9-12
Joint tape, mending, 9
Knee kicker, use of, 26
"Knock-apart" sashes, 35
Lamps
  sockets, replacing, 57
  switches, 61
Latches, door, problems of, 45
  patio doors, 47
Lath repair, 13
Lavatories
  drains
    assemblies, adjusting, 73
    clearing, 67
  sprays/diverters/aerators, 84
  See also Faucets